CONDUCT UNBECOMING

Set in the officers' mess of a regiment in India in the late 1800s. The two central characters, Drake and Millington, are young 2nd Lieutenants who have arrived to commence their probationary period of three months. Millington wishes to get out of the regiment as soon as possible in spite of his famous General father, while Drake is wildly enthusiastic and has complete faith in the honour of the regiment. Millington is accused of a crime, and, in secret court, Drake is subpoenaed to defend him. As the midnight sessions take place, Drake realizes that the regimental attitude is foul, Millington could not possibly have been guilty and his whole belief in the regiment is destroyed. After the final confrontation, Millington is fully exonerated and Drake resigns.

THE HEREFORD PLAYS

General Editor: E. R. Wood

Robert Ardrey	*Thunder Rock*
Robert Bolt	*A Man for All Seasons*
	The Tiger and the Horse
Harold Brighouse	*Hobson's Choice*
Coxe and Chapman	*Billy Budd*
Gordon Daviot	*Dickson*
Barry England	*Conduct Unbecoming*
J. E. Flecker	*Hassan*
R. and A. Goetz	*The Heiress*
H. Granville-Barker	*The Voysey Inheritance*
(Ed.) E. Haddon	*Three Dramatic Legends*
Willis Hall	*The Long and the Short and the Tall*
Fritz Hochwälder	*The Strong are Lonely*
Henrik Ibsen	*The Master Builder*
	An Enemy of the People
D. H. Lawrence	*The Widowing of Mrs Holroyd* and *The Daughter-in-Law*
Roger Macdougall	*Escapade*
Arthur Miller	*The Crucible*
	Death of a Salesman
André Obey	*Noah*
J. B. Priestley	*An Inspector Calls*
	Time and the Conways
James Saunders	*Next Time I'll Sing to You*
	A Scent of Flowers
R. C. Sheriff	*Journey's End*
J. M. Synge	*The Playboy of the Western World* and *Riders to the Sea*
Brandon Thomas	*Charley's Aunt*
Peter Ustinov	*Romanoff and Juliet*
John Whiting	*Marching Song*
	Saint's Day
	A Penny for a Song
Tennessee Williams	*The Glass Menagerie*
Oscar Wilde	*The Importance of being Earnest.*

BARRY ENGLAND

Conduct Unbecoming

with an introduction by
RONALD HAYMAN

HEINEMANN EDUCATIONAL
BOOKS LTD · LONDON

B

ß

Heinemann Educational Books Ltd
LONDON MELBOURNE EDINBURGH
TORONTO JOHANNESBURG
SINGAPORE AUCKLAND IBADAN
HONG KONG NEW DELHI
NAIROBI

ISBN 0 435 22270 8

First published 1971
Copyright © Barry England 1971

822
ENG

Published by
Heinemann Educational Books Ltd
48 Charles Street, London WIX 8AH
Printed in Great Britain by
Cox & Wyman Ltd
London, Fakenham and Reading

CONTENTS

INTRODUCTION

'Honour' is becoming a rare word in modern drama just as it is in modern conversation. In Shakespeare it recurs very frequently because honour is important as a motive. Henry V's heroism has its roots in his appetite for honour.

> But if it be a sin to covet honour
> I am the most offending soul alive.

The tragedy of Richard II is that his personality makes it impossible for his reign to be honourable.

> Mine honour is my life; both grow in one;
> Take honour from me and my life is done.

And it is not merely jealousy which drives Othello to kill his beloved Desdemona.

> An honourable murderer, if you will;
> For nought did I in hate, but all in honour.

It is only through his comic characters, like Falstaff, that Shakespeare can allow himself to poke fun at the notion of honour.

> Honour pricks me on. Yea, but how if honour prick me off when I come on? how then? Can honour set-to a leg? No. Or an arm? No. Or take away the grief of a wound? No. Honour hath no skill in surgery, then? No. What is honour? A word. What is that word, honour? Air. A trim reckoning! Who hath it? He that died o' Wednesday. Doth he feel it? No. Doth he hear it? No. It is insensible then? Yea, to the dead. But will it not live with the living? No. Why? Detraction will not suffer. Therefore I'll none of it: honour is a mere scutcheon: and so ends my catechism.

But this is far closer to today's attitude towards honour than the heroic attitude, and in our drama – which reflects our world – there are very few tragic heroes who die (or kill) for the sake of honour. In Robert Bolt's play, *A Man for All Seasons,* Sir Thomas More is very much a man of honour. When Henry VIII passes the Act of Supremacy, appointing himself Head of the Church of England 'so far as the Law of God allows', More accepts it but he chooses to die rather than take an oath to the Act of Succession.

> When a man takes an oath, Meg, he's holding his own self in his own hands. Like water (*cups hands*) and if he opens his fingers *then* – he needn't hope to find himself again.

But of course More is a historical character. The only modern tragic hero in a modern English play who dies for the sake of honour is Rupert Forster, the general, in John Whiting's *Marching Song.* As Shakespeare saw it, a King couldn't hope to rule without honour but in Whiting's view honour is a luxury that the modern ruler cannot hope to afford. It is because of this that the Chancellor in *Marching Song* was able to foresee the General's suicide.

> I knew him as a man to be very much like myself. But he'd something I've had to put away whilst I'm in office. Honour. So I knew what the end would be.

Barry England's *Conduct Unbecoming* is not a tragedy but it is a play about honour and it is significant that the word recurs in it so much. It is also significant that the action is set in the past – in India during the 1880s while the British Raj was still at the height of its powers. Formerly, before the Mutiny of 1857, it had been the British East India Company, originally a trading company, which had come in effect to be the ruler of India, but in 1858, after the British Army had fiercely suppressed the mutiny, the powers and territories of the company were formally transferred to the crown. Although the disaffection had originally been that of sepoys, not civilians, the ferocity of the reprisals had its effect on the whole country and the British Army in India was now more than ever like an occupying army in a defeated country.

Traditionally honour and the military career have been closely linked.

> I could not love thee (Dear) so much,
> Lov'd I not honour more

was the farewell of the Jacobean poet Lovelace to his mistress Lucasta, on going to the wars. But just how much did honour count for in the behaviour of the British Army in India after the Mutiny?

The word 'honour' is used, casually, several times in the early part of the play but the first time our attention is drawn forcefully to it is in the scene in which the Adjutant announces that Second-Lieutenant Millington, who has been accused of assaulting a lady, will be tried by a Court of Subalterns. When asked whether he is satisfied that the other young subaltern, Drake, should act as his defending counsel, Millington asks wryly whether he couldn't have the Colonel. When this question is received in silence he says

> Then I am content with Mister Drake. He is a gentleman of honour.

Just how accurate this assessment is, the action will show.

By now the contrast and the antipathy between the two young subalterns has been theatrically and very clearly established. Millington, the son of a general and the victim of an authoritarian upbringing, is trying to make the worst possible impression on the officers of the regiment in order to get himself dismissed and shipped back to England. Drake, the son of a major, is keen to make the best possible impression and from the moment when he and Millington arrived together, he has been apprehensive that Millington's calculated bad behaviour will reflect on him. He is therefore reluctant to take on the job of defending Millington and at first it looks as though he will have great difficulty in finding anything to say on his behalf. Later he even asks to be relieved of the embarrassing duty but it is the first interview he has with the Adjutant, who has given him the job, that indicates the play's main theme:

> ADJUTANT: It is very much a *fait accompli*, is it not?
> DRAKE: Still, it is, of course, my duty to defend Mister Millington in the best manner that I can. I see that now, sir.
> ADJUTANT: . . . Naturally you will find whatever you can to say in his favour.
> DRAKE: No, I mean to say, it is a matter of honour, is it not, sir? The honour of the Regiment demands that Mister Millington be properly defended.
> ADJUTANT: . . . As I say, it is necessary to go through the motions.

And that is all the Adjutant, who is convinced of Millington's guilt, expects him to do, to go through the motions, to play a role, to help to put on a show of justice, not to defend Millington to the best of his ability. When Drake gives signs of wanting to do more than is required of him, the Adjutant is not above putting pressure on him, first by reminding him that he is making a bad impression on the regiment and later by threatening to get rid of him.

Meanwhile Millington, who still wants to be sent back to England, is also applying pressure. He has no wish to be defended effectively and he refuses to collaborate. But Drake, who has never been in a position like this before, finds that he has more moral strength than he realized. If the honour of the regiment does not require that Millington be given a fair trial, then it certainly ought to, and once given the duty of siding with the maverick subaltern who has so successfully antagonized everyone else in the officers' mess, Drake is determined to do his best, at whatever cost. His sense of fair play gives him a sense of honour which acts as a yardstick against which the values of the regiment can and must be judged.

> ADJUTANT: You have finished yourself here, Mister Drake. Do you understand me. You are finished here.
> DRAKE (*sick at heart*): . . . If what I have seen in this courtroom . . .

is typical of the honour of this Regiment . . . then I shall be only
too happy to depart.

When the play began it looked as though it would be concerned with the probation of the two young subalterns. We
could see that Millington and Drake would both be on trial,
though we did not expect a courtroom scene in which there
would literally be a trial. Nor could it have occurred to us that
underneath the surface of the action it would be the regiment
that was on trial, with Drake not as defending counsel but as
judge. This is the irony of the title: it is actually the conduct of
the officers which is unbecoming.

Of course it is not only in the courtroom scenes that the
regiment is on trial but in the whole play. Barry England, who
has himself been a subaltern in the Far East, is anxious to be
fair, to show the credit as well as the debit side of the balance.
As characters, the officers are by no means entirely unsym-
pathetic. When we see them relaxing in the mess they may
seem rather juvenile in the way they talk about the polo
match and in their respect for discipline and tradition. They
all seem very anxious to be thought well of by each other, as
if life were an outsize rugger club. At the same time they are
spirited, they have glamour and panache and their camaraderie
is quite hearty and likeable, though we are compelled to acknowledge the streaks of cruelty in it. It is not only that men
of the Colonel's age look silly when seen trying to stab their
drawn swords into the hind-quarters of a stuffed boar on
rollers which is being pulled away from them as fast as it can
be dragged. When we see the game played in Act One, Scene
Two, we do not think of it as cruel. It causes pain to no one
except to the young officer with a gammy leg who is so keen
to prove himself to the others that he joins in the game when
he ought to be resting his leg. But later Drake reminds us that
the game originated in the field and that it gives play to a
cruelty which can also find its expression in bloodier ways.
The fact that it is played in the mess is linked by the action

to the fact that the officers of the regiment are willing to tell lies and to sacrifice Millington in order to protect a brother-officer who is capable of perpetrating the same outrage and cruelty on a living woman as is perpetrated in the game on a stuffed animal.

The play does not concern itself much with the army's treatment of the Indians. An Indian woman has been attacked with a sword but so has a white woman. There is talk about flogging sepoys before the Mutiny but one of the subalterns has been flogged too in the recent past and Millington is threatened with flogging. In other words Barry England treats British inhumanity towards the Indians in exactly the same terms as he treats British inhumanity towards the British. Altogether he has very little to say about the history of the British in India but the Indian background and the imperialist context are both apt for the play's examination of the army's values. So far as the action is concerned, the officers' main butt is Millington. Their behaviour towards him is anything but honourable and even Mrs Hasseltine, who is very much on their side and accuses Millington to protect one of them, ends up by calling them 'scum' and by describing Millington as

> the only gentle man I have met here in all my years with this Regiment.

The Colonel of the Regiment has been kept partly in the dark about what has been going on. Had he been told, he would have been forced to take action. At the same time, we are made to see that it is partly his own fault that he has been kept in the dark. His whole life has conditioned him to trust his brother officers unquestioningly. He is naïvely sincere when he says

> We do not – lie to one another in this Mess! Gentlemen do not question the honour of other gentlemen, Mr Drake!

And taking it for granted that Millington must be guilty, he tries to stop the trial. Not that there is anything dishonourable in the Colonel's own behaviour. Like the Adjutant, who finally gives Drake his full support, the Colonel never actively tries to suppress the truth.

When Drake stakes his honour on what he is saying, the Colonel allows the trial to continue, and when Drake proves his case, the Colonel is anxious not to lose him from the regiment.

> COL: I have this morning received your letter of resignation. Do you wish me to accept it, Mister Drake, or to tear it up?
>
> DRAKE: . . . I should like you to accept it. I am sorry, Colonel. I find that I cannot . . . put my honour on to a Regiment. Or on to a man. It is what I am . . . what I do.
>
> COL: . . . In a Regiment, it is necessary to put one's honour in trust.
>
> DRAKE: I understand that, Colonel.
>
> COL: Very well. I accept your letter of resignation, Mister Drake. (*Goes to veranda.*) . . . With regret.

It is not a regiment in which one can put one's honour in trust. Its values have been tried and found wanting. The subaltern who was so eager to be accepted by it is himself unable to accept it, whereas Millington, who wanted to get out, ends up by wanting to stay. And the Colonel, who seemed so self-satisfied and secure, surrounded by his admiring officers, ends up by looking forward to his retirement.

> I am the Regiment. What I have allowed to happen, is what I am. (*Slight pause.*) It is as well my time here is nearly done. You will not again speak to me of honour.

Formally, *Conduct Unbecoming* is not only a well-made play – in fact it is a 'whodunnit'. The excitement it offers in Acts Two and Three depends very largely on the gradual revelation that Millington was not the attacker who reduced Mrs Hasseltine to the state we saw her in at the end of Act One and the mystery of who the attacker was is cleverly sustained right up to the final curtain.

Besides having been in the army, Barry England has also been an actor, which means that he has learnt in a practical way what an actor and an audience need from a play-wright. He provides a rapid succession of swift-moving episodes full of spectacular action and scenes charged with a sense of occasion. He provides a theatrical and telling contrast between the dignified glamour of the military uniforms and the juvenile grossness of the game with the stuffed boar. He alternately fills the stage with a large ensemble of characters and thins the action down to two-handed and three-handed scenes. Above all he writes parts which give the actors fine opportunities. Even a good actor can make very little impression in a poor part and it is no accident that in the poll conducted by the magazine, *Plays and Players,* two of the drama critics picked out the actor who played Millington in the West End (Jeremy Clyde) as the Most Promising Actor of 1969 while another two critics picked out Paul Jones, who played Drake. And as the Best Play of the Year, two of the critics selected *Conduct Unbecoming.*

CAST OF FIRST LONDON PERFORMANCE

Conduct Unbecoming received its first performance at The Theatre Royal, Bristol on 20 May 1969 and transferred to The Queen's Theatre, London on 10 July 1969.
The play was presented by Donald Albery for Calabash Productions Ltd, with the following cast:

2ND LT EDWARD MILLINGTON	Jeremy Clyde
2ND LT ARTHUR DRAKE	Paul Jones
THE COLONEL, COLONEL BENJAMIN STRANG	
	Michael Barrington
THE SECOND IN COMMAND, MAJOR LIONEL ROACH	
	Peter Howell
MAJOR ALASTAIR WIMBOURNE, V.C.	
	Tony Steedman
THE DOCTOR, LT COL MAURICE PRATT	
	Martin Friend
THE ADJUTANT, CAPT RUPERT HARPER	
	Donald Pickering
THE JUNIOR SUBALTERN, 2ND LT	
RICHARD FOTHERGILL	Jonathan Elsom
LT FRANK HART	Rowland Davies
2ND LT JOHN TRULY	Ian Marter
2ND LT SIMON BOULTON	Gareth Hunt
2ND LT EDWARD WINTERS	Stewart Bevan
2ND LT FRANK HUTTON	Peter Smart
PRADAH SINGH, THE MESS MAJOR DOMO	
	Peter Bland
MESS HEAD WAITER	Sean Street
MRS MARJORIE HASSELTINE	Maxine Audley
MEM STRANG, THE COLONEL'S LADY	Gwynne Whitby

MRS BANDANAI	Saja Kumari
LAL, AN INDIAN SERVANT WOMAN	Cherina Mann
LADIES AT THE BALL	Lynne Moore
	Cherina Mann
	Vivienne Dixon
	Almond Plomley
WAITERS	John Guest
	Michael Hamilton
	Laurence Rooke

The play was directed by Val May, designed by Finlay James and the lighting was by Kenneth Vowles.

CHARACTERS

2ND LT EDWARD MILLINGTON
2ND LT ARTHUR DRAKE
THE COLONEL, COLONEL BENJAMIN STRANG
THE SECOND-IN-COMMAND, MAJOR LIONEL ROACH
MAJOR ALASTAIR WIMBOURNE, V.C.
THE DOCTOR, LT COL MAURICE PRATT
THE ADJUTANT, CAPT RUPERT HARPER
THE JUNIOR SUBALTERN, 2ND LT RICHARD
FOTHERGILL
LT FRANK HART
2ND LT JOHN TRULY
2ND LT SIMON BOULTON
2ND LT EDWARD WINTERS
2ND LT FRANK HUTTON
PRADAH SINGH, THE MESS MAJOR DOMO

MRS MARJORIE HASSELTINE, A WIDOW
MEM STRANG, THE COLONEL'S LADY
MRS BANDANAI, A WIDOW
LAL, AN INDIAN SERVANT WOMAN

INDIAN MESS WAITERS (4)
LADIES AT THE BALL (3)

TIME AND PLACE
India in the late Eighteen Hundreds
The ante-room to a British Army regimental officers' mess

THE SET

Those buildings that served the British Army in India as officers' messes were generally large, ornate of decoration, stolid of structure. The rooms were spacious, the furniture inclined to mahogany. It was not uncommon to find indigenous architectural extravagance wholly offset by imported conservatism.

The set represents the ante-room to an officers' mess. Its function is largely that of a club. It appears at first sight to be oppressive; not unlike a gloomy museum. There are portraits, showcases of medals, animals' heads stuffed and mounted, regimental colours. There are archways rather than doors.

Importantly (for they are incorporated into the action) there is a stone veranda upstage; a showcase within which is displayed a scarlet tunic on a dummy; a decorative gong; one portrait among the others of General Sir William Millington, V.C., late Colonel of the Regiment; and a chair, grander than the others, which is by tradition the preserve of the incumbent Colonel.

It is indeed *tradition* which is conjured by the set.

ACT ONE

SCENE ONE

Thunder of horses' hooves . . . Sound of drums . . .
The mess (the ante-room) afternoon.
DRAKE *enters, followed by* MILLINGTON. DRAKE *looks about*
as a man finally at peace. MILLINGTON, *with gloom.*
A silence.

DRAKE: Exactly as I imagined it would be.

MILLINGTON: How very uplifting for you.

DRAKE: I should hardly expect you to understand.

MILLINGTON: But I do, my dear fellow. You forget this
place has haunted my childhood too.

DRAKE: You appear to have learned little enough respect for it.

MILLINGTON: I've a very healthy respect for it. One should
always fear ghosts.

    DRAKE *stares at Regimental mementoes.*

DRAKE (*quietly*): It is like . . . coming home.

MILLINGTON: Isn't it, though? (*Notices, crosses to one of the
portraits.*) Good heavens. The Old Fellow himself.

DRAKE (*turns, crosses*): Your father?

MILLINGTON: Doesn't he look splendid?

DRAKE (*reads plaque*): 'General Sir William Millington, V.C.
Colonel of the Regiment, 1875–1881.'

MILLINGTON (*turns away*): Not to mention Order of the Bath.
(*Makes it sound absurd.*) Sheriff of the County, Justice of the
Peace . . .

DRAKE: You will find only military honours here. These are
past Colonels and holders of the Victoria Cross. That is the
Regimental tradition.

MILLINGTON: Ah.

DRAKE: As a General's son you will be expected to know these things.

MILLINGTON (*charming smile*): I can always turn to you for information, can't I?

Slight pause.

DRAKE: You will find no portrait of my father here. He was a Major.

MILLINGTON: But, my dear fellow. 'Backbone of the Mess.' How often have I heard the General say . . .

DRAKE (*abruptly*): We should present ourselves to the Adjutant.

MILLINGTON: If we can find him. Or indeed anyone.

DRAKE: Yes I . . . don't quite understand where everyone can be.

MILLINGTON: You don't suppose there's been another mutiny?

A silence.

DRAKE: I think I should warn you, Millington, that while I might, through force of circumstance, tolerate your imbecilities throughout our voyage together, you will find they are not appreciated here.

MILLINGTON: My dear fellow, we are not yet officially members of the Regiment. Won't you allow me a moment or two more of my native *joie de vivre*.

DRAKE: You realize, of course, that how you choose to behave will reflect on me?

MILLINGTON: Surely not?

DRAKE: There is no question of it. Unfortunately, we shall be judged together.

MILLINGTON: Oh, dear . . .

DRAKE: I should therefore tell you that I have every intention of making a success of my three months' probationary period with this Regiment, and joining it properly and fully at the end of that time.

MILLINGTON: That is kind of you, Arthur. There is, unhappily, a little matter I should perhaps share with you.

DRAKE: What is that?

MILLINGTON: I have no intention whatever of surviving my
  three months' probationary period. There is a ship, the
  Doric Castle, which sails for England in almost exactly three
  months to the day from now. I intend to be on her.

  Before Drake can react, PRADAH SINGH *enters. Stately,*
  dignified, sixties. He bows.

PRADAH: Good afternoon, Gentlemen. May I be of service?

DRAKE: You must be Pradah Singh.

PRADAH: And you, sir, are Mister Drake. If I may say, you
  are most like your father, under whom I had the honour to
  serve.

DRAKE: Thank you.

PRADAH: I had the honour to serve also under your father,
  Millington, sahib. Though I was, of course, much younger
  then, a mere boy.

MILLINGTON: Yes he did have me rather late in the day.

PRADAH: He was a fine gentleman, sahib.

MILLINGTON: So I am always being told.

DRAKE (*rescues Pradah*): I understand your father also served
  with the Regiment, Pradah Singh?

PRADAH: And my grandfather, sahib, in my family it is the
  tradition.

MILLINGTON (*clicks fingers*): Pradah Singh, I fancy I could do
  great service to a large whisky and soda. I wonder if you
  would be so kind . . .

DRAKE: That's quite out of the question.

MILLINGTON: In heaven's name, why?

DRAKE: We may neither order nor accept drinks until we are
  properly introduced into the Mess.

MILLINGTON: Good God. Now there is a point 'daddy' over-
  looked to mention.

PRADAH: I am sorry, sahib, it is the . . .

MILLINGTON: The tradition. Just so. Well, heaven send we
  be introduced soon.

DRAKE: Quite. Pradah Singh, we seem unable to locate the

Adjutant. Or indeed . . .

PRADAH: It is the polo, sahib. The end of season match against the Seventh Lancers.

DRAKE: Of course! I should have remembered!

PRADAH: The Colonel will be leading in the ladies soon.

DRAKE: We may yet have time to put in an appearance. It would be well received.

MILLINGTON: Tell me, Pradah Singh. Did you say there were to be ladies?

PRADAH: Yes, sahib.

MILLINGTON: Voluptuous ladies?

DRAKE: For God's sake, man!

The JUNIOR SUBALTERN *bustles on.*

JUNIOR SUB: Ah, there you are! Pradah Singh! A vast rapid stengah! We've about two minutes in hand!

PRADAH: Sahib.

JUNIOR SUB: What about you chaps?

MILLINGTON: Oh, my dear fellow. Just anything. I'm about to expire.

DRAKE: My companion is joking, of course. We're fully aware of the Regimental tradition.

JUNIOR SUB: Good. Splendid. Well done. Thank you, Pradah Singh.

PRADAH: Sahib.

PRADAH SINGH *withdraws.*

JUNIOR SUB: Damned silly these little tests. But one must be certain.

MILLINGTON: Oh, no . . .

JUNIOR SUB (*extends hand to Drake*): You must be Millington.

DRAKE: Er, no, no . . .

MILLINGTON: I have that dubious honour, my dear fellow.

JUNIOR SUB: Oh. Sorry.

They shake hands.

I'm Fothergill, Junior Subaltern. You're Drake, then.

DRAKE: Yes.

They shake hands.

JUNIOR SUB: Good. Well. Sit down, chaps. Lot to tell you, devil of a little time to tell it in.

MILLINGTON: We are allowed to sit?

JUNIOR SUB: Of course. Why not?

MILLINGTON: I just thought it might be another of those little tests. Pay no attention, please. (*Sinks into chair.*)

DRAKE: Mister Millington has a very personal sense of humour.

JUNIOR SUB: I see. Very funny. Yes. Ah, ha. You're sitting in the Colonel's chair, old man.

It is a moment before it dawns on MILLINGTON *that he is the guilty party. He springs up.*

MILLINGTON: Oh, great heavens! I shouldn't want to add sacrilege to my other crimes.

JUNIOR SUB: No. Quite. Now, I'm Fothergill, as I say, and it's my ...

MILLINGTON, *having backed to another chair, is peering over his shoulder at it. Hovering.*

JUNIOR SUB: Is something wrong, old man?

MILLINGTON: This ... isn't ... ?

JUNIOR SUB: No. No, it isn't.

MILLINGTON: No. Good. (*Sits, smiles at Drake.*) One is anxious to do the proper thing.

JUNIOR SUB: Quite. Now then. It's my job as Junior Subaltern to watch over you chaps for the next week or two. Make sure you understand what's what and so on. So let me remind you of one or two of the basic facts of life You don't speak to anyone, of course. Nor will anyone speak to you. Except me. It's my job to speak to you. And you may speak to me. But never to a senior officer – unless addressed first – in which case, you reply, 'Yes, sir'. Unless it is the Colonel, in which case you reply, 'Yes, Colonel'. We always call the Colonel, Colonel, in this Regiment.

DRAKE: Quite.

JUNIOR SUB: Quite.

MILLINGTON: That seems an eminently sound arrangement.

JUNIOR SUB: Yes, quite. Now then. When the Colonel arrives in a few moments with the ladies and the other officers . . .

MILLINGTON: Forgive me, my dear fellow, I have a query.

JUNIOR SUB: Well?

MILLINGTON: If we are not to speak, how are we to make our intentions known?

JUNIOR SUB: Junior officers do not have intentions.

MILLINGTON: . . . Suppose we should wish to leave the room?

JUNIOR SUB: I should try using the door, my dear fellow, we find that eminently satisfactory. But never before the Colonel, of course.

MILLINGTON: I do hope his bladder is weaker than mine.

JUNIOR SUB: I think you will find this whole operation will go a great deal more smoothly, Millington, if you remain silent. I should add that silence is a quality much admired in junior officers.

MILLINGTON: My dear fellow, I shan't utter another word.

JUNIOR SUB: Good. Excellent. Now, when the Colonel arrives, we shall withdraw to a corner over there. At an appropriate moment I shall strike the gong, announce Strangers in the Mess, and introduce each of you individually. No one will pay the least attention except the Colonel, who will say, 'Thank you, Mister Fothergill'. You will say nothing. We shall then wait for the Adjutant to join us, when you will present yourselves, and we shall withdraw to your quarters. Now, as to the ladies. In the Colonel's party this afternoon there will be, I think, only Mem Strang herself, the Colonel's lady and ah . . . Mrs Hasseltine.

The Junior Subaltern is plainly embarrassed.

DRAKE: The widow of Major Hasseltine.

JUNIOR SUB: Yes. Yes. I, ah . . . should perhaps say a word or two about Mrs Hasseltine.

Silence. He labours on.

She is a lady – much admired in the Mess. Very popular.
A – regular feature of our lives here. However. She is not
above – returning certain favours – particularly to younger
officers. Don't misunderstand me. She is very much a lady,
but . . .

DRAKE: Yes, of course. Most distressing . . .

MILLINGTON *is now fully attentive.*

JUNIOR SUB: Yes. Quite. My point is, junior officers
are well advised to remain – unsusceptible. She is a very
attractive woman. However, certain senior officers
having – you understand me? – 'made a point' with Mrs
Hasseltine . . .

DRAKE (*shocked, disapproving*): Oh. I see.

JUNIOR SUB: Of course this is a matter of which, while you
should be fully appraised, you know nothing.

DRAKE: No, quite.

JUNIOR SUB: Just remain – courteous, but . . .

MILLINGTON: Distant?

JUNIOR SUB: Distant, yes.

DRAKE: Enough is said.

JUNIOR SUB: Good. Good.

MILLINGTON: This . . . Mrs Hasseltine. She will be among us
this afternoon?

JUNIOR SUB: Briefly, yes. As I say we shall be withdrawing
to your quarters.

DRAKE (*firmly*): Quite.

MILLINGTON: Oh, quite.

An awkward silence.

JUNIOR SUB: The Lancers don't come to us for tea. We go
to them this evening.

DRAKE: Oh, by the way – who won?

JUNIOR SUB: We did. Four, three.

DRAKE: That is good news.

JUNIOR SUB: Yes. Major Wimbourne scored two absolutely
splendid goals in the last chukka.

DRAKE: Major Wimbourne, that's the V.C.

MILLINGTON *has wandered off, looking at Regimental trophies.*

JUNIOR SUB: The Regiment's third.

DRAKE: It's a magnificent record.

JUNIOR SUB: Unequalled.

JUNIOR SUBALTERN *tries to interest Millington.*

JUNIOR SUB: Your father was the Regiment's first V.C., of course, Millington.

MILLINGTON *is staring at a scarlet tunic, stained and torn, mounted on a dummy in a showcase. He doesn't turn, just murmurs.*

MILLINGTON: Yes.

JUNIOR SUB: Yes, well. I don't know if you have any other questions?

MILLINGTON: As a matter of fact, my dear fellow . . .

JUNIOR SUB: Yes?

MILLINGTON: I was wondering what on earth this filthy, scruffy old tunic can possibly be doing in the Mess?

Immediate outrage from the others. This is a calculated provocation.

JUNIOR SUB ⎱ : Mister Millington!
DRAKE   ⎰ : You know perfectly well, Millington!

JUNIOR SUB: That was Captain Scarlett's tunic! He was wearing it at the battle of Ratjahpur!

MILLINGTON: It must have been a very messy affair.

JUNIOR SUB: Warfare is not noted for its comfort, Mister Millington. Nor is the future of young officers who fail to acquaint themselves with the history and traditions of this Regiment. You hear me?! You will memorize and recite to me the known facts of the death of Captain Scarlett, who is a hero of this Regiment and will be honoured as such by you!

Silence. MILLINGTON *looks again at the tunic.*

MILLINGTON: Still, when you come to think of it, it must smell absolutely frightful.

JUNIOR SUB: Mister Millington!

PRADAH SINGH *enters with three waiters.*

PRADAH: The Colonel is just arriving, sahib, with the ladies.

JUNIOR SUB: Thank you, Pradah Singh. (*Turns away.*) Over here.

DRAKE: Pull yourself together, man!

MILLINGTON: But, my dear f...

DRAKE: I am being judged too!

JUNIOR SUBALTERN, DRAKE *and* MILLINGTON *withdraw to a corner as . . . the* COLONEL *enters with* MRS MARJORIE HASSELTINE, MEM STRANG, MAJOR WIMBOURNE, V. C. (*who is in polo gear with scarf*), *the* DOCTOR, *the* SECOND-IN-COMMAND, *The* ADJUTANT (*also in polo gear*), LT HART (*polo gear*), 2nd LTS WINTERS, BOULTON *and* HUTTON.

MRS HASS: I'm sure you are wrong, Colonel, I'll wager it is seven not six. What do you say, Mem?

MEM: Oh, I'm not much good at that sort of thing, I'm afraid, I'd have to look it up.

COLONEL: Lionel will know. Tell us, Lionel. How many matches are we up on the Lancers now?

ROACH: Seven, Colonel, counting today's.

MRS HASS: There you are. What did I say?

WIMBOURNE: We really will have to scratch that fixture soon, Colonel.

COLONEL: Oh, I don't think tradition is ever pointless, is it, Alastair?

WIMBOURNE: No, perhaps not.

DOCTOR: Besides, you enjoy whacking the pants off them, Alastair. You know damned well you do.

WIMBOURNE: How right you are, Doctor.

MRS HASS: Isn't he a clever boy, Colonel, to have scored two such beautiful goals?

WIMBOURNE: My dear Marge, I did it all for you!

COLONEL: Well he left it damned late in the day, I must say. What were you trying to do, Alastair, throw a scare into us?

WIMBOURNE: Thought I'd try to make the game more interesting for them, Colonel.

COLONEL (*laughs with others*): I don't think I'd mention that this evening if I were you.

WIMBOURNE: I promise I shan't.

COLONEL: We'll go straight out on to the veranda, Pradah Singh.

PRADAH: Very good, Colonel.

COLONEL: Marjorie, my dear . . .

    PRADAH SINGH *claps.* WAITERS *run on to veranda.* COLONEL *offers his arm to Mrs Hasseltine.* JUNIOR SUBALTERN *taps the gong. Everyone pauses.*

JUNIOR SUB: Colonel. There are strangers in the Mess, Colonel. May I present Mister Millington. And Mister Drake, Colonel.

    COLONEL *looks at them for a moment.*

COLONEL: Thank you, Mister Fothergill. (*To Mrs Hasseltine.*) As I was saying my dear . . .

MRS HASS: Surely that is never William Millington's boy? (*Glances back.*) He looks far too young.

    The COLONEL, *embarrassed, is about to speak, when* MILLINGTON *speaks.*

MILLINGTON: With respect, ma'am, I hardly believe you can have known my father. You also look far too young,

    A shocked silence. MEM *intervenes.*

MEM (*to* MRS HASSELTINE): Shall we, my dear . . .?

MRS HASS (*amused*): By your leave, Mister Millington.

MEM: Tell me, how are you getting on with that new gel of yours? What is her name . . .

    They go off on to the balcony. A pause. The COLONEL *follows, the others take their cue from him.*

COLONEL: How is young Truly, Doctor?

DOCTOR: Not too badly, thank you, Colonel. Be up and about in a day or two.

WIMBOURNE: Took a nasty knock. Played a damned fine game, though.

COLONEL: So did young Richard, I thought.

WIMBOURNE: He did, indeed, Colonel. Put that vital pass through to me in the last minutes . . .

They are off. The SECOND-IN-COMMAND, *last to leave, looks at Millington, at the Adjutant, frowns and departs. There remains only* ADJUTANT, *stiff with anger,* JUNIOR SUBALTERN, DRAKE *and* MILLINGTON.

ADJUTANT: Well, Mister Fothergill?

JUNIOR SUB: I'm sorry, Mister Harp . . .

ADJUTANT: I did not hear that, Mister Fothergill.

JUNIOR SUB: . . . I must have failed to make my instructions plain.

ADJUTANT: You are assumed to be capable of the duties of your office, Mister Fothergill. That is why you hold it.

JUNIOR SUB: Yes, Mister Harper.

A silence.

ADJUTANT: I am waiting, Mister Fothergill.

JUNIOR SUB: Present yourself, man (*to* DRAKE).

DRAKE (*smart pace forward*): I have the honour to present myself, sir. Mister Drake, sir.

ADJUTANT (*looks him up and down*): Thank you, Mister Drake.

MILLINGTON (*pace forward*): I also have the honour to present myself, sir.

ADJUTANT: Do you lack a name, sir?

MILLINGTON: Millington, sir.

ADJUTANT: Come here, Mister Millington.

MILLINGTON: Sir.

In silence, MILLINGTON, *subdued by this cold cutting, quiet man, goes to stand before him. Pause.*

ADJUTANT: If I hear from you again, it will be for the last time. Do you understand me?

MILLINGTON: May I be allowed to say . . .

ADJUTANT: Be silent, sir. Now have I made myself quite plain?

MILLINGTON: Yes, sir.

ADJUTANT: Return to your place.

MILLINGTON *goes.*

If you find your duties too arduous, Mister Fothergill, I can arrange to have you relieved of them.

JUNIOR SUB: No, sir.

ADJUTANT: That is all.

He goes. JUNIOR SUBALTERN *rounds on Millington.*

JUNIOR SUB: You bloody little fool! What the hell were you playing at?

MILLINGTON: I'm sorry, my dear fellow . . .

JUNIOR SUB: Be quiet! I told you to remain silent while there were senior officers in the Mess!

MILLINGTON: I certainly didn't mean to get you . . .

JUNIOR SUB: Will you be quiet, sir!? I don't know what the hell your game is, Millington, but let me tell you this! If you put up one more black against me, I'll make damned sure you're kicked out of this Regiment before you even finish your probationary period! Now you hear me!

MILLINGTON: Yes, Fothergill.

JUNIOR SUB: Mister Fothergill.

MILLINGTON: Mister Fothergill.

JUNIOR SUB: . . . Very well. Let's get you over to your quarters. Move!

They go, JUNIOR SUBALTERN *last. A volley of horses' hooves.* WAITERS *rearrange furniture as required . . .*

The Mess. The Mess Night.

PRADAH SINGH *claps hands, the* WAITERS *run off.* HEAD WAITER *stands by drinks table on veranda. The* SECOND-IN-COMMAND *and* JUNIOR SUBALTERN *come on, both in duty dress with swords.*

ROACH: Well, Richard. Brandy?

JUNIOR SUB: Please, sir.

ROACH: Two brandies, please, Pradah Singh.

PRADAH: Sahib.

    PRADAH SINGH *signals to* WAITER, *who brings them to him on a tray.*

ROACH: Well, sit down, my boy.

JUNIOR SUB: Thank you, sir.

    They sit.

    Offstage – laughter, hunting cries come close.

    (*Smiles.*) Sounds as if the Game's in full cry, sir.

ROACH: Yes. (*Smiles.*) One of the penalties of being Officer of the Day on a Mess Night, um?

JUNIOR SUB: Well, it's better than being Officer of the Week, sir. At least I shall be free for the Ball on Saturday.

ROACH: Well, I shan't pretend that I mind too greatly about that.

    PRADAH SINGH *brings drinks.*

PRADAH: Your brandy, sahib.

ROACH: Thank you, Pradah Singh.

PRADAH: Sahib.

JUNIOR SUB: Thank you.

ROACH: Your health, Richard.

JUNIOR SUB: And yours, sir. Thank you.

    They drink.

    Offstage: A sudden loud burst of shouting and laughter, very close. Then LT HART *runs in from stage right, dragging behind him what is in fact a stuffed boar on wheels, with a handle by which he pulls it. He runs across and off left shouting . . .*

HART: Oink, oink – Chaaaaarrge!

   Almost at once the pursuing body comes through after him. WIMBOURNE *and* ADJUTANT (ADJ. *from veranda*) *in the lead, closely followed by* HUTTON, BOULTON, WINTERS, COLONEL – *and the* DOCTOR, *trailing, out of condition.* ALL *are in Mess Dress: They carry drawn swords and charge across, off left.*

WIMBOURNE: There he goes . . . !

HUTTON: This way, sir . . . !

ADJUTANT: After the devil . . . !

WINTERS: Which way did he go . . . ?

BOULTON: Down towards the flagstaff . . . !

WINTERS: Chaaaaarrge . . . !

COLONEL: Up the Regiment . . . !

DOCTOR (*puffing*): My word, Colonel, we'll have to find someone slower next time . . . !

JUNIOR SUB: I rather think the Doctor's past his best for the Game, sir!

ROACH: Well, I suppose it is his job to keep us fit, rather than himself, um?

   Now LT TRULY *hobbles on from the right, far behind, limping, wobbling about and panting.*

TRULY: Which way did they go?!

JUNIOR SUB: Down towards the flagstaff, old man!

TRULY: Ah! Charge . . . ! (*Hobbles left, waving sword.*)

ROACH: For heaven's sake, Truly – don't damage that leg of yours any further.

TRULY: Never fear, sir! Charge . . . ! (*He hobbles off left.*)

JUNIOR SUB: Johnny's a goer, sir.

ROACH: Yes. Richard, I wanted to ask you about your two new charges. Has there been any improvement there?

JUNIOR SUB: Not much, sir. He let the Colonel's new string of ponies escape yesterday.

ROACH: Millington.

JUNIOR SUB: Yes, sir. We got them together again. By nightfall.

ROACH: It won't do. Won't do.

JUNIOR SUB: Couldn't we – get rid of him, sir?

ROACH: Of course we could. Wouldn't look good though, would it? General's son. Colonel of the Regiment . . .

JUNIOR SUB: Still, it makes it awkward for us, sir – having to discipline him, without . . .

ROACH: Oh, don't worry. The Colonel will kick him out soon enough if he has to. Simply better not, if it can be avoided.

JUNIOR SUB (*unconvinced*): Yes, sir.

　　Offstage: Sounds of the 'hunt' circling the Mess.

ROACH: Extraordinary business. Richard, did you notice Millington was drinking too much at dinner?

JUNIOR SUB: Yes, sir. But strictly speaking, there's no ruling about that, sir. As long as he can hold it.

ROACH: All the same, I think you should remove him as quickly and quietly as you can, from the Mess tonight.

JUNIOR SUB: Right, sir.

　　HART *comes charging through again, dragging the boar,* ADJUTANT, WIMBOURNE *and* WINTERS *close at his heels.*

WIMBOURNE: Nearly got him . . . !

HART: Hell . . . !

　　HART *skids and falls. The* OTHERS *at once close round the boar, sinking swords into its hind-quarters.*

WIMBOURNE: Aha –yes. (*Sinks in sword.*) A point!

ADJUTANT (*stabs*): A point!

WIMBOURNE (*stabs again*): A veritable point!

WINTERS (*stabs*): Hooray!

　　The joke is evidently to stab the boar only in the hind-quarters, this being the area presented in 'flight'. DRAKE *and* MILLINGTON *have now appeared on the veranda, watching* HART *scramble up as the* OTHERS *stab and stab again.*

HART: Hey – hang off, you chaps!

WIMBOURNE: A point!

ADJUTANT: And another!

HART: You're cheating!

WINTERS: Another!

WIMBOURNE: What do you mean, cheating?

HART: I slipped, I fell!

ADJUTANT: Stay on your ruddy feet, then!

HART: To hell with you, then!

> HART *seizes the handle, starts off again.*

WIMBOURNE: Aha – he's away . . . !

ADJUTANT: Charge . . . !

> *They start in pursuit.*

COLONEL: No, no, gentlemen, I pray you . . . ! Your Colonel is old – too old . . .!

WIMBOURNE: Never, Colonel.

ADJUTANT: Perish the thought, Colonel.

WINTERS: Shame, Colonel.

BOULTON: Shame.

COLONEL (*panting, chuckles*): I thank you for your kind thoughts, gentlemen. But really, the Doctor and I are quite exhausted for this evening. Eh, Doctor?

DOCTOR: I must second the motion, Colonel. (*Sinks into chair.*) I prescribe – drinks for the Mess.

COLONEL: An excellent suggestion. Pradah Singh.

PRADAH: Very good, Colonel.

> PRADAH SINGH *motions to* WAITERS, *who serve the company.* PRADAH SINGH *will only serve* COLONEL, WIMBOURNE *and* ROACH, *and assist senior officers with cigars.* HART *takes the boar off, the others give their swords to waiters.*

COLONEL: Well, Lionel . . . Alastair . . . what was the final score?

HART (*quickly*): It was a draw, Colonel!

WIMBOURNE: A draw? What the blazes do you mean, a draw, sir?

ADJUTANT: It was a walkover, Colonel – six valid points at least!

WIMBOURNE: At least six – more like a dozen.

HART: But I fell down!

WIMBOURNE: You shouldn't drink so much, then.

Laughter, all very good-natured this argument.

HART: Colonel, sir – I appeal to you. Surely it doesn't count if the runner falls down, Colonel?

WIMBOURNE: Of course it does!

ADJUTANT: Why ever shouldn't it?

HART: A ruling, Colonel.

COLONEL: I'm not gifted with the wisdom of Solomon, gentlemen.

Cries of 'Shame'.

Lionel, a ruling is required on the Mess Sport.

ROACH: Well, Colonel, I suggest . . . 'Should the runner be incapacitated, there shall be allowed – during the period of his incapacitation – one valid point only'.

HART: Hear, hear!

WIMBOURNE: Lionel, that is disgusting.

ADJUTANT: ⎫ Shame . . . !
AND   ⎬ Shame . . . !
OTHERS: ⎭ Shame . . . !

HART: Carried unanimously, Colonel!

COLONEL: Very well, Mister Hart. I declare a draw.

HART: Thank you, Colonel.

WIMBOURNE: Well anyway, it was a damned fine run.

TRULY *limps on during 'Hear, hear's'.*

TRULY: Did you catch him all right?

WIMBOURNE: Where the devil have you been?

ADJUTANT: Making an inspection of the lines, have you, John?

TRULY: I've got a handicap, dammit.

COLONEL: Come on, young Truly, sit down – you'll ruin that leg of yours.

TRULY: It's perfectly all right, Colonel, I assure you.

WIMBOURNE: Don't argue with the Colonel, you young puppy. Come on!

WIMBOURNE, *massively strong, lifts* TRULY *as though he were no weight at all and dumps him, gently in fact, into a chair – to a cheer and laughter. There is much warmth and affection in all this boisterousness. This is their world.* DRAKE *and* MILLINGTON, *down left now, are very much out of it, though* DRAKE *tries to appear in.*

TRULY: Thank you, sir!

MILLINGTON (*clutches Drake's arm, sotto*): What an absolutely extraordinary performance, my dear fellow.

DRAKE (*brushes arm away*): Be quiet.

MILLINGTON: Don't take your arm away . . . (*He is very, very drunk, but not obviously so.*)

COLONEL: Well now, Adjutant, I think it's about time the young officers entertained the old codgers . . .

WIMBOURNE: Hear, hear . . .

DOCTOR: Splendid idea, Colonel . . .

ADJUTANT: I'm sure Mister Boulton would be happy to oblige us with a dramatic recitation, Colonel.

WIMBOURNE (*claps*): Approbation for Mister Boulton, gentlemen . . .

They all clap, laughing. SECOND-IN-COMMAND *motions to* JUNIOR SUBALTERN *who works around towards Millington.*

BOULTON: Oh, I say, look here, it was me last time. What about Johnno?

TRULY (*clapping*): Gammy leg, old man.

WIMBOURNE: Carry on, Mister Boulton . . .

BOULTON (*desperate*): Well – what about the new chaps?

JUNIOR SUBALTERN *having reached Millington tries to get him to leave.* MILLINGTON *obstinate.*

WIMBOURNE: There's a thought . . .

BOULTON: Yes . . .

WIMBOURNE: Colonel. Have I your permission to call upon the new men?

ROACH: Perhaps a little soon, Colonel . . .

COLONEL: Oh, I don't see why, Lionel. It is Plassey Week, after all. Yes, go ahead, Alastair, why not . . .?

WIMBOURNE: Colonel. You, sir – forward march. (*Points to centre stage.*) Here.

It is, of course, Millington, though he doesn't take it in.

JUNIOR SUBALTERN *hisses at him.*

JUNIOR SUB: Go on, man – move!

MILLINGTON *lurches slightly, advances with the stiff formality of the very drunk.*

WIMBOURNE: Come on, sir – double time.

MILLINGTON: Sir. (*Stands facing Wimbourne.*)

WIMBOURNE: Address yourself to the Colonel, sir.

MILLINGTON: Yes, sir.

MILLINGTON *faces Colonel. His eyes have the very open earnest stare. His reactions are just a little delayed. The others have drunk enough to miss this.*

MILLINGTON: Colonel, sir.

COLONEL: What is your name, sir.

MILLINGTON: Millington, sir.

COLONEL: Millington. Yes. General Millington's boy.

MILLINGTON: Yes, sir. Colonel.

COLONEL: Well, we want you to entertain us, Mister Millington. What are you going to do?

Silence.

COLONEL: Um? Well? Speak up, speak up.

MILLINGTON (*solemnly*): Sing a song, Colonel.

COLONEL: A song. All right. Good. Carry on, Mister Millington.

MILLINGTON *straightens, takes a deep breath, shuts his eyes and sings.*

MILLINGTON: 'Plaisir d'amour . . .'

WIMBOURNE: It's a bloody Froggy song. (*Laughter.*)

MILLINGTON: 'ne dure qu'un moment.'

ADJUTANT: Sing up, Mister Millington!

OTHERS *call out too.*

MILLINGTON: 'Chagrin d'amour dure toute . . .'

HART: Louder!

BOULTON: Sing louder!

MILLINGTON: 'la vi — — — — — — c.'

WINTERS: Let's hear you, Mister Millington!

ROACH: Shh . . .

COLONEL: Be quiet, gentlemen . . .

Throughout this traditional barracking, MILLINGTON *has sung on, oblivious, as he now does, in a sweet, clear, perfect voice.*

MILLINGTON: 'J'ai tout quitte pour l'ingrate Sylvie; Elle me quitte et prend un autre amant.'

They listen in absolute stillness and silence now to the sweet voice in the night.

'Plaisir d'amour

ne dure qu'un moment:

Chagrin d'amour dure toute

le vi — — — — — — c.'

MILLINGTON *draws the final notes right away into nothing. Silence. Stillness. A shifting, almost of embarrassment. Then the* COLONEL *taps gently in applause on the arm of his chair.* OTHERS *do the same.* WIMBOURNE *applauds properly with his hands as do* SUBALTERNS.

COLONEL: Well done, Mister Millington.

DOCTOR: Well sung.

WIMBOURNE: Well sung indeed, young man.

ROACH: Very good, Mister Millington.

Visible relief from SECOND-IN-COMMAND, DRAKE *and* JUNIOR SUBALTERN.

MILLINGTON: Colonel, sir.

COLONEL: Yes, Mister Millington?

MILLINGTON: Permission to pass out, Colonel.

He drops like a stone at the Colonel's feet. Dead drunk. Shocked, stunned silence.

COLONEL (*rises, turns away*): Well, really!

ROACH (*rising*): Mister Harper!

ADJUTANT: Mister Fothergill!

JUNIOR SUB: Yes, sir!

ADJUTANT: Remove this officer to his quarters, sir!

JUNIOR SUB: Yes, sir!

ADJUTANT: I shall speak to you in the morning, Mister Fothergill.

JUNIOR SUB: ... Sir.

> DRAKE *and* JUNIOR SUBALTERN *bend over* MILLINGTON – *they will carry him out. Only now does* COLONEL *turn back, angry and contemptuous.*

COLONEL: Perhaps you'd join me on the veranda, Lionel?

ROACH: Thank you, Colonel. I should like that.

DOCTOR (*disgusted*): Gentlemen who cannot hold their liquor shouldn't drink.

WIMBOURNE (*rather amused*): He did finish his song, Doctor You will allow him that. (*He laughs.*)

COLONEL: I do not find it amusing, Alastair.

WIMBOURNE (*to attention*): I'm sorry, Colonel.

> *Bravely,* HART *steps in.*

HART: Colonel, sir.

COLONEL: Yes, Mister Hart?

HART: May I have the honour to challenge you to a match at billiards, Colonel?

> *Silence.* THEY *wait the Colonel's reaction.*

COLONEL: Very well, young man. (*Turns to go off right.*) If you want another caning.

WIMBOURNE: I'll lay a pony on the Colonel.

HART: What about me?!

COLONEL: Now, Alastair. You know we don't allow gaming in the Mess.

WIMBOURNE: No, Colonel.

COLONEL: Not in front of the Colonel, anyway.

WIMBOURNE (*grins*): No, Colonel.

TRULY: Colonel, sir.

COLONEL: Yes, Mister Truly?

TRULY: Permission to fall out, Colonel.

COLONEL: Leg troubling you?

TRULY: Just a bit, Colonel.

COLONEL: Get to bed, then.

TRULY: Thank you, Colonel.

COLONEL: Doctor, I'd much appreciate it if you'd take a look at . . .

TRULY gives a cry and staggers.

DOCTOR: Of course, Colonel.

TRULY: Sorry, Colonel! (*In evident pain.*)

Slightest pause. WIMBOURNE *strides across.*

WIMBOURNE: Come on, young man!

He gathers him up into his arms.

TRULY: It isn't necessary, sir, I assure you.

WIMBOURNE: Be quiet, sir. Where do you want him, Doctor?

DOCTOR: His own quarters, I think.

WIMBOURNE: Right! With your permission, Colonel.

COLONEL: Thank you, Alastair.

WIMBOURNE strides out, carrying TRULY.

COLONEL: Well, Mister Hart. Let's see if you've learned anything since our last encounter.

HART: Right, Colonel.

About to go off right, the COLONEL turns back halting the DOCTOR at left, across stage.

COLONEL: Oh, Doctor.

DOCTOR: Yes, Colonel?

COLONEL: Perhaps you'd better take a look at the other young gentleman.

DOCTOR: Very well, Colonel.

They go off.

LIGHTS FADE, WAITERS tidy chairs, strike glasses, etc.

LIGHTS CHANGE TO early morning setting.

The MESS. *The next morning.*

MILLINGTON *limps on, heavily hung over, pale-faced and taut he gathers his strength to call.*

MILLINGTON (*a whisper*): Pradah Singh . . . (*He clears his throat and tries again.*) Pradah Singh . . . !

    PRADAH SINGH *enters.*

PRADAH: Good morning, sahib.

MILLINGTON: Whisky, Pradah Singh. Large, large . . .

PRADAH: If I may say, with respect, sahib. It is a trifle early . . .

MILLINGTON: Don't make me argue, there's a good fellow.

PRADAH: No, sahib.

    MILLINGTON *is too still. Concerned* PRADAH SINGH *fetches drink.*

    Your whisky, sahib.

    Hands trembling, MILLINGTON *takes drink, gags on it, gets it down. His body shudders as the 'shakes' depart. A silence.*

MILLINGTON: I needed that.

PRADAH (*sadly*): Yes, sahib.

MILLINGTON (*sharply*): Thank you, Pradah Singh.

    PRADAH SINGH *withdraws as* DRAKE *comes on, at the end of his tether, coldly enraged.* MILLINGTON *re-adopts his flippant manner.*

DRAKE: Where the devil have you been, Millington? I've been searching everywhere for you.

MILLINGTON: My dear fellow, good morning.

DRAKE: You realize we're due here at eight for the Junior Subaltern.

MILLINGTON: I am here, Arthur.

DRAKE: Don't be flippant with me!

MILLINGTON (*winces*): . . . I wish you wouldn't shout, my dear chap.

    Pause.

DRAKE *(turning away)*: Why did you ever come here, Millington?

MILLINGTON: Oh, one cannot escape one's destiny, my dear fellow. One must go through the motions of failure.

DRAKE: Then let me warn you, Millington. I have never in my life wanted anything but to be a part of this Regiment. I do not intend to have that ambition destroyed by you. If necessary I shall resort to physical means to protect it. Do you understand me?

MILLINGTON: My dear fellow, you are never referring to fisticuffs, surely.

DRAKE: What do you think I am referring to, Mister Millington? Or do you imagine there is a particular dispensation that protects the sons of Generals?

MILLINGTON: Of course I do not.

DRAKE: Do you not, Mister Millington?

MILLINGTON: Certainly not, Arthur.

DRAKE: It has never entered your head, that were you anyone but a General's son, you would be on a ship by now and bound for home?

MILLINGTON: That can't be true.

DRAKE *(turns away in disgust)*: Of course it is.

    Pause. MILLINGTON *shaken.*

MILLINGTON: . . . My God, that's awful.

DRAKE *(cruel, amused)*: . . . It is also rather amusing, is it not, Mister Millington? Your plans to quit this Regiment may prove more sanguine that you had imagined.

MILLINGTON *(stunned pain)*: . . . How much farther have I got to go?

    The JUNIOR SUBALTERN *storms on. Where Drake has been bitingly cold, he is ablaze with anger.* MILLINGTON *appears dazed.*

JUNIOR SUB: Millington! Come here! Come here!

MILLINGTON: . . . Yes, Mister Fothergill.

JUNIOR SUB: Move, man! Move!

    The JUNIOR SUBALTERN *trembles with anger. When*

MILLINGTON *stands before him, he raises his cane just short of Millington's face. One feels he might at any moment strike.*
I have just been up before the Adjutant because of you!
Now once more, Millington – once more – so help me, I will give you such a thrashing – you hear me – ? Within an inch of your life!

MILLINGTON (*subdued*): Yes, Mister Fothergill.

JUNIOR SUB (*seizes Millington's jacket*): Come here! (*Drags* MILLINGTON.) Come here, Millington! I want to show you something.

He pitches MILLINGTON *almost off his feet, up on to the veranda, where he throws him against an upright and, from behind, yanks* MILLINGTON's *head round by the hair so that he looks off right.*
Now you see it!? Do you, Millington?! You see that – that structure?! That frame?!

MILLINGTON: Yes, Mister Fothergill.

JUNIOR SUB: That is a whipping post, Mister ͵Millington! That is where they flogged sepoys in '57! And that is where you're going to find yourself, Mister Millington! You understand me?! You hear me?! Out there! In that frame!

This disturbs Drake. It goes too far. MILLINGTON *covers face with hands, starts down from the veranda, the* JUNIOR SUBALTERN *pushes him in passing,* MILLINGTON *falls on his knees down stage.*

JUNIOR SUB: You hear me?! Do you?!

MILLINGTON *opens his hands. He has been covering not fear, but a terrible sweet smile. He chuckles slightly.*

MILLINGTON: Oh, my dear fellow . . . The whip holds no terror for me. No terrors at all.

Chilling. Silence. JUNIOR SUBALTERN *quieter, colder, comes down.* DRAKE *uncomfortable.*

JUNIOR SUB: We'll see, Mister Millington. We'll see.

DRAKE (*disturbed*): . . . Mister Fothergill was speaking – figuratively of course.

JUNIOR SUB: Mister Fothergill was speaking literally, Mister

Drake. The whip has been used on a difficult subaltern in recent times. No doubt it will be again.

DRAKE: ... I see.

MILLINGTON: Who was the lucky man?

JUNIOR SUB: That does not concern you. Now listen to me, both of you. The Adjutant has instructed me to inform you officially, that if he receives one more report of unsatisfactory behaviour by either one of you, that man's service will be terminated at once. You, Mister Millington, will cut down on your drinking. As to the Ball tonight, the Colonel has reluctantly given permission for you to wear Mess Dress. You will prove yourselves worthy of that honour. You will both now put on your best jodhpurs and tunics and report to Sergeant-Major Lang. The stables need mucking out. Move.

DRAKE: Mister ...

JUNIOR SUB: Move!

MILLINGTON: Yes, Mister Fothergill ...

LIGHTS FADE *to evening setting. Music ...*

The MESS. *The night of the Ball.*

Music from up off left. The Ball is in progress on the plain, situated mainly up left offstage. WAITERS *enter from right carrying large, lighted chinese lanterns which they hang on the veranda.*

One WAITER *carries a lighted candelabra to the drinks table down left. He fetches a tray of champagne and begins pouring it out. Three young ladies enter from right and are met by* HART *who kisses their hands.* WAITERS *take their wraps and they exit left followed by* HART. ALL OFFICERS, *including* MILLINGTON *and* DRAKE, *wear full mess dress,* OFFICERS *above and including the* ADJUTANT *wear Regimentals – except the* SECOND-IN-COMMAND, *Officer of the Week and* HART, *Officer of the Day.* HART *and* SENIOR OFFICERS *wear swords.* SUBALTERNS *do not. The women are beautifully gowned.*

Open with a shout of laughter, and a group – WIMBOURNE, TRULY, BOULTON, WINTERS, HUTTON, *of which* MRS HASSELTINE *is the centre of attraction, comes on to the veranda.*

WIMBOURNE: You're an outrageous woman, Marge!

WINTERS: It's a damned funny story, though, sir, you must admit!

WIMBOURNE (*amused*): And you, sir, are far too young! Get away! Get away!

MRS HASS: Now you really must allow me a moment or two to rest, gentlemen.

BOULTON: Shame!

TRULY: Shame!

WINTERS: May I have the pleasure of the first dance on your return, ma'am?

WIMBOURNE: Insubordination, sir!

MRS HASS: You're too young. Your squadron Commander says so.

WIMBOURNE: Quite right, Marge.

BOULTON: Is one ever too young to appreciate wit and beauty, Mrs Hasseltine?

MRS HASS: For that, I might consider it.

WIMBOURNE: You lecherous young devil. Away with you – the pack of you!

Jokingly he draws sword and waves it about his head. SUBAL-TERNS *retreat laughing.* COLONEL *comes on to the veranda.*

COLONEL: In heaven's name, Alastair. You're not decapitating our subalterns, are you?

WIMBOURNE (*sheaths sword*): Defending a lady's honour, Colonel.

MRS HASS: A pardonable exaggeration, Colonel.

COLONEL: You're a wicked woman, Marge, but you look splendid.

MRS HASS: I hope to remain so, Colonel, but your young gentlemen won't release me.

COLONEL (*with mock severity to Subalterns*): What are you young gentlemen doing here? The Second-in-Command and I have scoured the countryside in search of partners for you. All of the most eligible and attractive young ladies in the district await you on the plain.

BOULTON: You're never referring to the 'Crows', Colonel?

COLONEL: To your duties, gentlemen. Quick march.

BOULTON: Oh Lord! Bags I the one with the red hair! (*Dashes off left.*)

WINTERS: Hey! Wait a bit, she's mine!

Dashes after Boulton, TRULY *hobbling in the rear. Music starts again, rather quieter.*

WIMBOURNE: I know just how they feel, Colonel.

COLONEL: We met a goodly number of what may fairly be termed 'crows' ourselves, did we not?

WIMBOURNE: We did indeed, Colonel. It's Marge, she's spoiled them for anyone else.

MRS HASS: Oh! Alastair. I should hate to think I'd spoiled anyone for anything. Or vice versa.

MEM: Colonel.

WIMBOURNE: Good evening, Mem.

MEM: Good evening. Colonel, dear, the guests . . .

COLONEL: Yes, yes, duty calls. I think we owe the ladies a turn or two, Alastair – if you will excuse us, my dear.

MRS HASS: Of course, Colonel.

WIMBOURNE: Sorry, Marge.

MRS HASS: Don't be silly. They all want to dance with our dashing V.C.

WIMBOURNE: Won't you come with us?

MRS HASS: No, no, I think I'll sit out here, and watch you ah . . . doing your duty with the 'crows'.

WIMBOURNE: Oh Lord! Now there is an act deserves a medal if you like.

MRS HASS: Get away with you!

WIMBOURNE: Shan't be long.

> WIMBOURNE *exits,* MRS HASSELTINE *wanders on to the veranda.* A WAITER *enters from left with a tray of drinks, at the same time* MILLINGTON *enters from right and stops him.*

MILLINGTON: I say, just a moment, my dear fellow.

WAITER: Sahib . . .

> MILLINGTON *takes a drink. The* WAITER *attempts to move on.* MILLINGTON *stops him. He downs first drink, returns glass. Takes second, downs that, replaces glass. Takes third and fourth, bows.* WAITER *bows.*

WAITER: Sahib . . .

> MILLINGTON *goes to put aside fourth drink as* WAITER, *leaving via veranda, passes* MRS HASSELTINE.

Mem sahib?

> *She takes a drink.* WAITER *goes.* MILLINGTON *turns. His charm is too calculated in this scene, too evidently scheming. Her attitude is ambiguous when not imperious.*

MILLINGTON: Why . . . Mrs Hasseltine.

MRS HASS: Mister Millington, I believe.

MILLINGTON: Your servant, ma'am.

MRS HASS (*glancing outside*): You should be out dancing,

Mister Millington. There are many young ladies on the plain would be glad of your company.

MILLINGTON: Tell me, ma'am. I know they reverence the cow in India. Do they also reverence the crow?

MRS HASS (*amused*): Some of them are very attractive.

MILLINGTON: It is pleasing, ma'am, to hear beauty pay tribute to mere attractiveness.

MRS HASS: . . . Do you not think you have already paid me one compliment too many in public, Mister Millington?

MILLINGTON: That is why I am taking such care to pay my future compliments to you in private, ma'am.

MRS HASS: You are to pay me no more compliments at all, Mister Millington. At least, none that you could not as readily pay your mother.

MILLINGTON: Ah, well, she, poor lady, is dead.

MRS HASS: I am sorry.

MILLINGTON: You have no reason to be, Mrs Hasseltine. (*Looks at portrait.*) It is a compliment to her good sense.

He makes a slight toast to portrait. She follows his gaze.

MRS HASS: You know, you really shouldn't drink so much, Mister Millington.

MILLINGTON: No, ma'am. No, I shouldn't.

MRS HASS: Particularly in the circumstances.

MILLINGTON: Ah. My reputation travels before me.

MRS HASS: It is already quite extensive.

MILLINGTON (*smiles*): . . . I should like to think that we had something in common, Mrs Hasseltine.

MRS HASS: It is a great mistake, Mister Millington, to be deceived by reputations.

MILLINGTON: But a common one, Mrs Hasseltine. (*Looks again at portrait.*) Sadly common.

MRS HASS: . . . That is the second slighting remark you have made of your father.

MILLINGTON: Thoroughly well merited, I do assure you. He was a perfect swine.

MRS HASS: That is not an attitude you will find appreciated

here, Mister Millington. The General is revered in this Mess.

MILLINGTON: It was not a pronouncement to the Mess, Mrs Hasseltine, but an aside to you.

MRS HASS: Under the impression, apparently, that it would fall on sympathetic ears.

MILLINGTON: My sole impression of you, Mrs Hasseltine, is that you are a woman.

MRS HASS: Don't be insolent, Mister Millington.

MILLINGTON: Forgive me. I had not thought the remark insolent. I so wanted to make a good impression. Clearly you must have taken to him.

MRS HASS: I scarcely knew your father. He was a hard man. But never without cause.

MILLINGTON: I think you do him an injustice, Mrs Hasseltine. I don't remember that he ever flogged me himself. We had an estates manager, Mister Radlett, who was adept at that particular function. A fine, free-flowing action.

MRS HASS: I doubt it was more than you deserved.

MILLINGTON: I cannot argue with that, ma'am. (*Chuckles.*) What is amusing is that they are proposing to repeat the dose here. Did you know? Yes. Out there, on that frame thing – strapping me up and walloping away.

MRS HASS: I should derive what amusement you can from it now, Mister Millington. They will certainly do it if you compel them to.

MILLINGTON: I'm sure of that, ma'am.

MRS HASS: What they have done before, and recently, they will do again.

MILLINGTON: What has escaped me, thus far, is the identity of the victim of that last occasion.

MRS HASS: . . . It was Mister Truly.

MILLINGTON: Ah. He of the gammy leg. No wonder he is such an example to us all.

MRS HASS: Let us hope he will prove an example to you, Mister Millington.

MILLINGTON: Let us hope so. He must have done something spectacularly wicked to have been accorded such a privilege.

MRS HASS: He behaved stupidly towards me.

MILLINGTON (*quietly*): Yes. Yes, I wondered about that. (*Looks up and smiles.*) Dear me. It appears that I shall have to restrain myself.

MRS HASS: Yes, Mister Millington, you will.

MILLINGTON: It won't be easy, ma'am.

MRS HASS: Steel yourself . . . Good night, Mister Millington.
    She turns to go.

MILLINGTON (*sharply*): No! (*Quickly smiles.*) No . . . Don't go. Please.

    Music stops offstage. Clapping. 'Plaisir d'amour' starts up softly.

    (*Wandering about.*) Did you know, it is said that when two pigeons mate, they mate for life?

MRS HASS: Really.

MILLINGTON: Yes, so I have read.

MRS HASS: How touching, Mister Millington.

MILLINGTON: I must say I find it rather sad.

MRS HASS: Why?

MILLINGTON: Imagine if one were to die before the other.

MRS HASS: That is why you drink. For the lost pigeon.

MILLINGTON (*smiles*): No, ma'am.

MRS HASS: Why, then?

MILLINGTON (*with a sweet smile*): Because I can't stop.

MRS HASS: Is that – true?

MILLINGTON: Oh, don't concern yourself about it, please.

MRS HASS: How old are you?

MILLINGTON: Nineteen.

MRS HASS: Then you have all . . .

MILLINGTON: 'All life is before me', that's what they say.

MRS HASS: . . . Well. You come to us laden with advantages, do you not?

MILLINGTON: But to you, it seems, I come with none. (*Moves towards her.*) Am I quite out of favour?

MRS HASS (*turning to go again*): Good night, Mister Millington . . .

MILLINGTON (*grabbing her arm*): Please. Mrs Hasseltine . . .

MRS HASS: No. You will do yourself no good with this.

MILLINGTON: As to that. We may differ.

    Voices of the COLONEL *and* WIMBOURNE *approach
veranda.*

MRS HASS: Stay away from me!

WIMBOURNE (*off*): What do you think – is he right, Colonel?
Will there be trouble on the Frontier?

COLONEL (*off*): Bound to be sooner or later, Alastair.

    MRS HASSELTINE *has broken free and sweeps on to the
veranda as* COLONEL *and* WIMBOURNE *come on.*

Ah, there you are, Marjorie.

MRS HASS (*overbright*): Duty done, Colonel?

COLONEL: For the moment, my dear, yes. You take Alastair
away and dance with him. It's my turn for a brief respite.

MRS HASS: With pleasure, Colonel.

    MRS HASSELTINE *and* WIMBOURNE *leave veranda.*
COLONEL *comes down steps, sees Millington and stops. He
is sitting in Colonel's chair.*

COLONEL: Good evening, Mister Millington.

MILLINGTON (*leaps to his feet*): Good evening, Colonel.

    The COLONEL *looks for rescue, but there is none.* MILLING-
TON *at first enjoys Colonel's discomfiture. A long silence.*
(*In this scene underlying developing ambiguity of mood.*)

COLONEL: You, ah, enjoying yourself, Mister Millington?

MILLINGTON: Thank you, Colonel, yes.

COLONEL: Good, good.

    Silence. COLONEL *goes to table and picks up cigar box. Feels
compelled to offer one to Millington.*

COLONEL: Do you, ah . . . ?

MILLINGTON: No thank you, Colonel.

COLONEL: Very wise, very wise . . .

MILLINGTON: Allow me to offer you a light, Colonel.
(*Crosses.*)

COLONEL: Oh, er, thank you. Thank you.

  COLONEL *lights cigar from* MILLINGTON*'s match.*

Thank you, Mister Millington.

MILLINGTON: They say a good subaltern always carries a box of matches and a spare handkerchief to a Ball, Colonel.

COLONEL: Quite right. Quite right.

MILLINGTON: My father told me.

COLONEL: Yes, yes.

  Silence.

We, ah, we were all very sorry to hear of his death, you know. He was a fine man.

MILLINGTON: He was, Colonel. A great loss to the nation at large.

COLONEL: Just so. Just so. (*Looks at portrait.*) Sadly missed by all who knew him.

MILLINGTON: Sadly, Colonel, sadly.

COLONEL: Well. You bear a fine name, Mister Millington.

MILLINGTON: I do, Colonel, I do.

COLONEL: Yes.

  DRAKE *comes on. Stops short.*

DRAKE: Oh. (*Comes to attention.*) Good evening, Colonel.

COLONEL: Mister Drake.

  Silence.

COLONEL: Well. Carry on, carry on . . . (*Heads relieved for the veranda.*)

MILLINGTON: It's been a great pleasure, speaking with you, Colonel.

COLONEL (*stops and turns*): . . . And you, Mister Millington. And you.

  He escapes. Yet this last exchange might almost have been sincere.

DRAKE: What the devil have you been playing at?

MILLINGTON: My dear fellow. Just a little chat with the Colonel, nothing more.

DRAKE: Are you drunk?

MILLINGTON: Now is that kind, Arthur?

DRAKE: Are you?

MILLINGTON: I may have had one or two . . . (*Goes to veranda.*)

DRAKE: I think it's about time we retired to our quarters.

MILLINGTON: I say, do you think we should; before the Colonel?

DRAKE: I will get permission . . .

MILLINGTON: Very well, Arthur. Sleep well. I'm off dancing . . . !

He is gone before DRAKE *can stop him.*

DRAKE: Wait . . . Millington! Wait!

He pursues Millington. Cries offstage and the girl with red hair runs on, laughing in mock fear from the veranda to down left pursued by BOULTON *riding* HUTTON *horseback, brandishing a parasol, like a lance. She runs right and then off left.* BOULTON *and* HUTTON *collide in the entrance with the* SECOND-IN-COMMAND. HART *with a lantern enters right.*

ROACH: Gentlemen, gentlemen . . .

BOULTON: Sorry, sir.

HART: Time for the inspection, sir.

ROACH: Yes, Frank, I'm afraid you and I must return to duty. I'm sorry to deprive you of the charms . . .

HART: Oh, that's all right, sir. Fair shares. Somebody else's turn this year.

ROACH: Turn . . . ?

HART: Well, sir. She is an annual affair . . .

ROACH: Oh, I see . . . Very well, we'd better begin. We'll start at the East gate and work our way round to the picquets . . .

They exit. LIGHTS *change to early morning setting.*

Music changes to 'Early one Morning'. TRULY *and a girl cross from veranda left, go off right – followed by* WINTERS *with a girl also.*

Soft sounds of night . . .

The MESS. *The Ball. Early morning.*

The COLONEL *comes on, tired, looking his age. As he crosses stiffly to his chair,* PRADAH SINGH *comes on.*

PRADAH: May I fetch anything for you, Colonel.

COLONEL: No. No, thank you, Pradah Singh. I am in need of a new pair of legs.

PRADAH: I shall endeavour to see that you are not disturbed, Colonel.

COLONEL: Thank you, Pradah Singh.

> PRADAH SINGH *goes on to the veranda. The* COLONEL'S *eyes close.* MEM STRANG *comes on to the veranda,* PRADAH SINGH *indicates the Colonel. She smiles.* PRADAH *exits and* MEM *goes down to sit beside the Colonel.*

MEM: I thought you were feeling a little tired, Colonel dear.

COLONEL: Oh, Mem . . . (*Struggles to rise.*)

MEM: No, no, don't get up.

COLONEL (*sinks back*): If you will forgive me, my dear.

MEM: I'd forgive you anything.

COLONEL: What time is it?

MEM: Nearly two.

COLONEL: We ought to be able to leave soon. I feel we've said good night to most of our guests already.

MEM: There are just the usual late stayers . . . Marjorie, of course . . . Mister and Mrs Hopwood . . . That major in the Lancers.

COLONEL: Peregrine Forster . . .

MEM: And his wife . . . It's been a lovely Ball.

COLONEL: Has it, Mem?

MEM (*looks at him*): Yes.

COLONEL: . . . It's something one feels – one owes to the Past.

MEM: I know. (*A pause.*) Colonel, dear?

COLONEL: Um?

MEM: Would you do something for me?

COLONEL: What?

MEM: All evening I have danced with bounding young men and doddering old bores. I should so like to dance with my own dear husband.

COLONEL: Oh, dear. Must I?

MEM: It's an order.

COLONEL: Very well . . .

> COLONEL *and* MEM *rise. Offstage there is a curious sound – a muffled cry.*

What was that?

MEM: What, dear?

COLONEL: Extraordinary . . . I thought I heard . . . Come along, my dear.

MEM: Thank you, Colonel.

> *Offstage – a deep scream of terror and pain.*

It's Marjorie . . . !

MRS HASS: Help . . . ! Help me . . . ! Help me . . . !

> MRS HASSELTINE *scrambles on all fours on to the veranda – making mindless noises – hair dishevelled – dress torn.*

WINTERS (*off*): What the devil was that!

COLONEL: Pradah Singh!

MRS HASS: Ah . . . ! Ah . . . ! Ah . . . !

> PRADAH SINGH *runs to her from veranda left, crouches, trying to lift her.* MEM *has reached her.* WINTERS *and* BOULTON *run on from right, so does* DRAKE. *The music has stopped.*

MEM: My dear! What's happened?!

> MRS HASSELTINE *clings to her.*

MRS HASS: Mem . . . ! Mem . . . !

MEM: It's all right, it's all right, it's all right . . .

> MRS HASSELTINE *is in total terror. The* OTHERS *mutter stupid things: 'What's happened?' etc.*

COLONEL: Pradah Singh – brandy. Quickly.

PRADAH: Yes, Colonel.

> WIMBOURNE *runs on from left.*

WIMBOURNE: What the devil's happened?

> HART *and* JUNIOR SUBALTERN *enter.*

BOULTON: It's Mrs Hasseltine. She's . . .

COLONEL: Let's get her to a chair, shall we?

MEM: Give me a hand, will you, Alastair, lift her . . .

WIMBOURNE: What's happened?

WINTERS: She's been attacked . . .

> ADJUTANT *and* ROACH *enter.* WIMBOURNE *helps* MRS HASSELTINE *to a chair, centre.*

MRS HASS: Alastair.

ROACH: What's happened?

WIMBOURNE: It's all right, Marge, it's all right . . .

> *The others are grouping round, the* DOCTOR *pushing through.*

DOCTOR: Let me through, please, gentlemen . . .

COLONEL: Let the Doctor through, gentlemen . . .

> PRADAH SINGH *gives brandy to* MEM.

PRADAH: Brandy, Mem sahib . . .

MEM: Thank you. Drink this, dear . . .

DOCTOR: What on earth has happened, Mem?

MEM: She's been attacked, Doctor . . .

> MILLINGTON *now appears on empty veranda, rubbing his head behind the ear. He looks bemused, slightly drunk.*

DOCTOR: Let me see, my dear . . . Let me just see . . .

WIMBOURNE: Who by? That's what I want to know! Who did it?

> MRS HASSELTINE, *looking about wildly, suddenly points at Millington.*

MRS HASS: It was him! It was him!

MILLINGTON (*vaguely*): What . . . ?

> WIMBOURNE *makes for him.*

WIMBOURNE: My God, you little . . .

COLONEL: Alastair!

> *They freeze at his tone. He turns formally to the* SECOND-IN-COMMAND.

Major Roach. This officer is under arrest!

ROACH: Mister Harper, detail two officers!

ADJUTANT: Mister Fothergill, Mister Hart!

    HART *and* JUNIOR SUBALTERN *advance on* MILLINGTON
– *who smiles* . . .

CURTAIN

ACT TWO

SCENE ONE

The MESS. *The next evening.*

The JUNIOR SUBALTERN, HART, WINTERS, BOULTON, TRULY *and* HUTTON *and – rather apart –* DRAKE *are waiting subdued. Silence. After a moment,* BOULTON *crosses to veranda.*

BOULTON (*murmurs*): . . . What do you think they'll do?

WINTERS (*shrugs*): Court Martial, I should imagine.

BOULTON: Well, he bloody well deserves it.

JUNIOR SUB: There is another possibility.

WINTERS: What?

JUNIOR SUB: The Adjutant may convene a Subalterns Court.

TRULY: What's that?

JUNIOR SUB: Well, there hasn't been one for some time . . .
    (*Sees* ADJUTANT *approaching.*) Attention, gentlemen!
        They rise. The ADJUTANT *enters. Silence.*

ADJUTANT: Good evening.

ALL: Good evening, sir.

ADJUTANT: Be seated, gentlemen.
    He goes upstage. They sit.
    He waits for complete silence.
    Then he turns.

ADJUTANT: This matter is to be settled by Subalterns Court Martial. I shall explain to you in a moment exactly what that entails. Suffice it to say that – fortunately for us – Mrs Hasseltine is agreeable that this matter should remain within the confines of this Regiment. Provided it is dealt with by us. Which it will be. Mister Fothergill.

JUNIOR SUB (*rises*): Sir.

ADJUTANT: Bring in the accused officer.

JUNIOR SUB: Sir.

JUNIOR SUBALTERN *goes off. Silence. Returns with* MILLINGTON *who enters first.*

MILLINGTON: Thank you, my dear fellow.

JUNIOR SUB: The accused officer, sir.

ADJUTANT: Sit down, Mister Millington.

MILLINGTON *sits in a chair previously placed by* TRULY. JUNIOR SUBALTERN *returns to place.*

ADJUTANT: You are to be tried by Subalterns Court Martial. I shall now explain that. A Subalterns Court consists of five officers. One President, and four members. There will also be one officer prosecuting, and one defending. Verdict will be by vote of five. (*A pause.*) A Subalterns Court Martial has no official existence, gentlemen. It is outside the normal structure of discipline and command. Should a Senior Officer become officially aware of it, he would be obliged to end it. However, make no mistake. The powers of this court are summary and absolute. There is no appeal to higher authority. Do I make myself plain?

General murmurs of 'Yes, sir'.

Now as to witnesses. You may, by tradition, require any officer of whatever rank to appear before you. You may also call civilian personnel. But, should you choose to call a senior officer, gentlemen, his appearance before this court will in no way affect his official knowledge of these proceedings, which do not exist. Do you understand me?

Murmured acknowledgement. MILLINGTON *shakes his head, amused chuckle at this doubletalk.*

ADJUTANT: I do not think you will find this amusing for long, Mister Millington. The Court will convene in this ante-room at midnight tonight. And on whatever subsequent nights may be required to arrive at a verdict. Pradah Singh will be on duty. But you will neither acknowledge nor address him. The Court will be composed as follows, The President, myself. The members, Mister Boulton, Mister Hart, Mister Winters and Mister Truly. The Prosecuting Officer will be Mister Fothergill. The Defending Officer, subject to the Accused Officer's approval, will be Mister Drake. Are there any questions?

> MILLINGTON *looks amused at the shocked Drake*.

MILLINGTON: Am I to understand that I have some option in the matter?

ADJUTANT: Stand up, Mister Millington.

> *A moment, then* MILLINGTON *rises*.

You are entitled if you wish, to select some other officer to defend you.

MILLINGTON: I suppose I couldn't choose the Colonel? No. Well, then I am content with Mister Drake. He is a gentleman of honour.

ADJUTANT: That is praise indeed. Are there any further questions?

DRAKE (*rises hesitant*): Sir . . .

ADJUTANT: Mister Drake?

DRAKE: Am I . . . obliged to accept this duty?

ADJUTANT: . . . Mister Millington has chosen you, Mister Drake.

DRAKE: . . . Yes, sir. (*He sits again.*)

ADJUTANT: You will now return to your duties, gentlemen. You, Mister Drake, will remain here. Mister Millington will wait outside under escort. Mister Hutton.

> *They depart, coming to attention, leaving. 'Sir'.* MILLINGTON, *amused by* DRAKE, *goes also. A pause.*

ADJUTANT: I appreciate that you have been under something of a disadvantage since you arrived here, Mister Drake. But it is necessary that Mister Millington be defended. Traditional forms must be observed.

DRAKE: It is simply that I am anxious to do well here, sir.

ADJUTANT: Of course. But there are many ways in which one may serve the Regiment, Mister Drake. I don't think you need fear to find yourself guilty by association.

DRAKE: It was wrong of me to raise the matter, sir.

ADJUTANT: Not at all. Any young subaltern would appreciate your dilemma. Though I hardly think that, in this particular instance, you will need to embarrass yourself unduly. It is very much a *fait accompli,* is it not?

DRAKE: Still, it is, of course, my duty to defend Mister Millington in the best manner that I can. I see that now, sir.

ADJUTANT: ... Naturally you will be required to find whatever you can to say in his favour.

DRAKE: No, I mean to say, it is a matter of honour, is it not, sir? The honour of the Regiment demands that Mister Millington be properly defended.

ADJUTANT: As you say, it is necessary to go through the motions. But there. You are no fool, Mister Drake. You know what is required of you.

DRAKE: ... To be fair, sir.

ADJUTANT: Just so. To be fair. To the Regiment. Good. Excellent. Carry on, Mister Drake.

He goes. DRAKE *frowns: a moment of unease. The arrival of* MILLINGTON *hardens him.*

MILLINGTON: Can I come in, my dear chap? I do hope he persuaded you to take on my case, Arthur.

DRAKE: You are determined to make life impossible for me here, aren't you?

MILLINGTON: For myself, my dear fellow. Not for you.

DRAKE: I pray God you have at last succeeded.

MILLINGTON: Amen to that, old man.

Pause.

DRAKE: I don't know how you can expect me to defend you. I've no sympathy for you whatever.

MILLINGTON: I understand that isn't necessary.

DRAKE: I know nothing of courtroom procedure.

MILLINGTON: For this particular charade, I doubt you'll need to.

DRAKE: You'll get a fair trial, Millington! A damned sight fairer than you deserve!

MILLINGTON: My dear Arthur. With you to defend me, how can I fail?

DRAKE (*pause*): ... You had better tell me what happened.

MILLINGTON: I wouldn't want to shock you, Arthur.

DRAKE: For God's sake!

MILLINGTON: I, ah, endeavoured to touch her.

DRAKE: Where?

MILLINGTON: In the Folly.

DRAKE (*furious*): Now look, Millington . . .

MILLINGTON: My dear fellow . . .?

DRAKE (*controls himself*): . . . Just tell me what happened.

MILLINGTON: There's little enough to tell, Arthur. I am, as you know, anxious to absent myself. When I saw Mrs Hasseltine go into the Folly, it seemed an admirable opportunity to, ah – if you'll pardon the expression – combine business with pleasure. So I . . . endeavoured to come to grips with her. Without, it must be admitted, any marked success.

DRAKE: You forget, Millington, I saw Mrs Hasseltine when she came into the Mess.

MILLINGTON: My dear fellow, I saw her before she went into the Mess. She was quite unimpaired, I assure you.

DRAKE: Her dress was torn. She was in a state of hysteria.

MILLINGTON: Perhaps she tore it on the shrubbery. Does it really matter?

DRAKE: Exactly how much of this assault can you remember?

MILLINGTON: My dear Arthur, it was an assault only in the most technical sense, I do assure you.

DRAKE: You were drunk, weren't you?

MILLINGTON: Not that drunk.

DRAKE: Enough to have no clear recollection of what occurred.

MILLINGTON: My dear fellow, I'm never that drunk. You've seen what happens when I drink too much. I go down like a felled ox. There's nothing for me between clarity and oblivion.

DRAKE: If you are to be believed . . .

MILLINGTON: In heaven's name, what does it matter? I'm guilty, Arthur. I admit it.

DRAKE: I doubt you'll be permitted to in the courtroom.

MILLINGTON: Whyever not?

DRAKE: You'll be obliged to plead not guilty. That is customary to ensure a fair hearing.

MILLINGTON: Well, my dear fellow, by all means let us plead not guilty, but let us have an end to the matter as rapidly as we may.

Drake is filled with contempt.

DRAKE: You are very proud of yourself, aren't you, Millington?

MILLINGTON: . . . It was necessary.

DRAKE: Necessary. To assault an older woman, simply in order to . . .

MILLINGTON: In heaven's name, anyone would think I'd raped the blasted female.

DRAKE: Didn't you?

MILLINGTON: My dear Arthur, I took hold of her arm, she pulled away, I took hold of it again – and wallop! She did me more damage than I her.

DRAKE: How so?

MILLINGTON: Well, look, my dear fellow. (*Pulls right ear forward.*) I've a gash that must be every bit of two inches long.

DRAKE: . . . That is the work of Mrs Hasseltine?

MILLINGTON: It certainly isn't the work of myself.

DRAKE: How did she do it?

MILLINGTON: She hit me, Arthur.

DRAKE: With what?

MILLINGTON: I haven't the faintest idea. It felt at the time like the Cawnpore cannon. Laid me out cold.

DRAKE: I see. And that was for touching her on the arm?

MILLINGTON: My dear Arthur—

DRAKE (*disgusted*): You're lying, Millington.

MILLINGTON: Well, if you wish to believe me guilty of having raped her up hill and down dale, it really doesn't make any difference, does it?

DRAKE: And those are the grounds on which I am to defend you, are they? That in fact you did nothing?

MILLINGTON (*smiles*): . . . Are you sure you have properly understood the Adjutant's instructions, Arthur? Those are the grounds on which you are to fail to defend me.

DRAKE: Oh yes. You would like to believe that, wouldn't you?

MILLINGTON: I'm easily satisfied, Ar . . .

DRAKE: Well, you'll get a fair trial, Millington! I shall see to that! Much as I should prefer to prosecute you, I shall defend you to the utmost of my ability! For I at least have some conception of where my duty lies! However repugnant that duty may be to me.

MILLINGTON: . . . You, ah, you won't exceed requirements, will you, Arthur? You know, you could do yourself a great deal of good here.

DRAKE: Get out of here. You make me sick.

MILLINGTON: Well, no matter. I fancy you will find there is little you can do for this particular lost cause. Au revoir, my dear fellow. See you at the witching hour.

MILLINGTON *goes.* DRAKE, *alone, is angry, uncertain. He marches off. Lights fade to a night setting. At* PRADAH SINGH's *direction waiters come on to arrange furniture for the courtroom. Upstage, long table, five chairs. Stage right, Prosecution table and chair. Stage left, Defence table and chairs (two). Stage centre, witness chair. The lights come up.*

SCENE TWO

The MESS. *Midnight. The* TRIAL.
PRADAH SINGH *claps hands.* WAITERS *run off.* MILLINGTON
enters, crosses to PRADAH SINGH.

MILLINGTON: Good evening, Pradah Singh.
   There is no reaction from Pradah Singh. DRAKE *enters
   right with papers.*
DRAKE: Pradah Singh. (MILLINGTON *makes a face.*) I . . .
   understand that I am not to address you. But . . . could you
   tell me please where we sit? (*Very nervous.*)
PRADAH (*indicates*): The Defence is seated here, sahib.
DRAKE: Thank you.
PRADAH (*sympathy: indicates*): The Court, sahib. The Pro-
   secution. The Witness, sahib.
DRAKE: Thank you, Pradah Singh.
PRADAH: Sahib.
   He goes. DRAKE *crosses to Defence table and drops one of his
   papers.*
MILLINGTON (*amused*): You appear nervous, Arthur. (No
   reply.) Well, you are on trial, too. Are you not? (DRAKE
   ignores him, sits and starts writing.) What are you doing, my
   dear fellow?
DRAKE: I am endeavouring to find some points to make in
   your favour.
MILLINGTON: Oh, do let me see. (*Looks over Drake's
   shoulder.*) 'One, drink. Two, size.' Size of what, Arthur?
   'Three . . . Character of Mrs Hasseltine, question mark.' I
   think I'd forego that one, if I were you. 'Four . . .' What, no
   four? Is that the sum of my virtues, Arthur?
   HUTTON *enters.*
HUTTON: Stand up!
   They rise. The members of the Court file on. BOULTON *first,*
   ADJUTANT *last. Eventually they stand behind their chairs. At*

centre upstage table: HARPER *centre;* HART, *then* BOULTON *to his left.* WINTERS *then* TRULY *to his right.* JUNIOR SUB-ALTERN *goes to Prosecution table. A silence.*

ADJUTANT: Be seated, gentlemen. (*He sits last.*) This Court is now in session. Mister Millington, rise.

With a look at Drake he does.

Mister Hart.

HART (*rises*): Mister President. The charge before this Court reads as follows. (*Reads from a sheet.*) 'That on the seventeenth instant, the accused officer, Second Lieutenant Millington, E. serving with this Regiment, did attack, wound and assault Mrs Marjorie Hasseltine, then a guest of this Regiment, the widow of the late Major Robert Hasseltine, also of this Regiment. That in this, as in his prior actions, he has grossly insulted his brother officers, he has betrayed the trust reposed in him by his Colonel and his brother officers, he has brought the name of this Regiment into dishonour and disrepute, and he has conducted himself in a manner unbecoming an officer and a gentleman.' The charge ends, Mister President. (*He sits.*)

ADJUTANT: How do you plead, Mister Millington? Guilty or not guilty?

MILLINGTON: Indifferent, Mister President.

DRAKE (*rises quickly*): The accused officer pleads not guilty, Mister President.

ADJUTANT: . . . Not guilty, Mister Drake?

DRAKE: . . . Well, yes, Mister President.

ADJUTANT: I see. You, Mister Millington, will remain silent, or these proceedings will be continued in your absence. Do you understand me?

MILLINGTON: Yes, Mister President.

ADJUTANT: Sit down. (MILLINGTON *sits.*) Both of you. (DRAKE *sits.*) Mister Fothergill.

JUNIOR SUB: I am ready to call my first witness, Mister President.

ADJUTANT: Carry on.

JUNIOR SUB: I call the Doctor.

ADJUTANT: Mister Hutton.

HUTTON, *who is sitting by the door, rises, goes out right and returns with the* DOCTOR.

HUTTON: Would you come in, please, sir.

DOCTOR: Of course. (*Enters.*) Mister President.

ADJUTANT: Be seated, Doctor, please.

DOCTOR: Thank you. (*Sits in witness chair.*)

ADJUTANT (*smiles*): I am obliged to remind you, sir, that you are on your honour to speak the truth.

DOCTOR: Of course, Mister President.

ADJUTANT: Thank you, sir. Mister Fothergill.

JUNIOR SUB (*comes from desk*): Doctor, on the night of the seventeenth a Ball took place which was interrupted by . . . a most unfortunate incident. Did you examine Mrs Hasseltine later at the hospital?

DOCTOR: I did indeed, yes.

JUNIOR SUB: Had she been attacked?

DOCTOR: Most certainly. There is no question of that.

JUNIOR SUB: In a serious manner, Doctor?

DOCTOR: In my opinion it was a most gross and cowardly assault.

JUNIOR SUB: I see. And did Mrs Hasseltine give any indication, in your presence, of who might have been responsible?

DOCTOR: She did, yes. She made a direct accusation.

JUNIOR SUB: Against whom, sir?

DOCTOR: Against that officer.

JUNIOR SUB: And were Mrs Hasseltine's injuries such as to sustain this accusation, Doctor?

DOCTOR: Well, injuries are not in themselves evidence as to the identity of the attacker. However, Mrs Hasseltine repeated her accusation at my specific request. In front of Major Wimbourne, this morning.

JUNIOR SUB: How did that come about, Doctor?

DOCTOR: I wanted to be certain in my own mind that she was not acting while still in a state of hysteria. I pointed out that it was an extremely serious charge to bring against a young officer.

JUNIOR SUB: But she repeated the charge?

DOCTOR: She did, yes. Most emphatically.

JUNIOR SUB: Thank you, Doctor. Finally I should like to ask whether when you examined Mister Millington, as I believe you did this morning – whether you found anything to indicate that he might have been responsible for this attack?

DOCTOR: You are referring to the gash on his head?

JUNIOR SUB: I am, yes.

DOCTOR: Well, Mister Millington himself admitted to me that it was Mrs Hasseltine who had struck him.

JUNIOR SUB: Struck him when, Doctor?

DOCTOR: As I understand it, during the course of a struggle.

JUNIOR SUB: Are you saying that Mister Millington admitted to you that he had attacked Mrs Hasseltine?

DOCTOR: So far as I am aware, he has freely admitted that to anyone who has asked him.

    MILLINGTON *nods agreeably.*

JUNIOR SUB: I see. Thank you, Doctor. (*Returns to place.*)

ADJUTANT: Mister Drake?

    DRAKE *rises. Nervous. Anxious to do what he imagines is required of him. Hesitant.*

DRAKE: Mister President . . . Gentlemen of the Court . . . Doctor . . .

DOCTOR: Mister Drake . . .

DRAKE: You, uh, you have referred to the . . . injuries sustained by Mrs Hasseltine.

DOCTOR: I have, yes.

DRAKE: . . . I am not clear . . . in my own mind . . . exactly what they amount to.

DOCTOR: Well . . . She was bruised about the wrists and arms. The palms of her hands were skinned. The legs also, down here (*shins*). The knees were bruised. She was otherwise cut about the body. Her dress was torn . . .

DRAKE: . . . Would it be fair to say that . . . many of these injuries might have been sustained in . . . running through the trees and shrubbery that surround the Folly?

DOCTOR: I think it would be fair to say that, yes. Though it must be added that she was only running because she had been attacked.

ADJUTANT: Just so, Mister Drake.

DRAKE: Yes, Mister President. Had she been . . . in any other sense . . . interfered with, Doctor?

DOCTOR: Do you mean sexually?

ADJUTANT: Mister Drake. Mister Millington is not charged with rape, but with assault.

DRAKE: Yes, Mister President.

ADJUTANT: Very well. The Court does not require an answer to that question, Doctor.

DOCTOR: Mister President.

DRAKE (*at a loss*): . . . Well, would it be fair to say, that this was . . . relatively speaking . . . an unsuccessful attack?

ADJUTANT: It is of no concern to this Court, Mister Drake, whether Mister Millington succeeded or failed in what he intended to do. It is the attempt with which he is charged.

DRAKE: I was merely trying to suggest, Mister President, that there might be some mitigation in the fact that he failed.

DOCTOR: But he did not fail, Mister Drake. One cannot measure the effects of an assault of this kind purely in physical terms.

ADJUTANT: Exactly so, Doctor.

DOCTOR: The shock to the nervous system – to the emotions of the patient is extreme. You saw for yourself, Mister Drake. Mrs Hasseltine was in a state of terror – bordering, in my opinion, on acute hysteria.

ADJUTANT: The Court finds no mitigation in the circumstance you describe, Mister Drake.

DRAKE: No, Mister President. (*Pause.*) But I am not clear, Doctor . . . as to exactly why . . . Mrs Hasseltine was so afraid.

DOCTOR: I cannot believe that is a serious comment, Mister Drake.

DRAKE: I mean to say, Mister Millington is not a large man, sir. On the day you examined us, you said that you would have to 'put some meat on him'.

ADJUTANT: We appear to have strayed yet again from the purpose of these proceedings, Mister Drake.

DRAKE: Well, it is surely relevant, Mister President, that Mister Millington is hardly capable of any serious assault on Mrs Hasseltine, particularly if he were affected by alcohol at the time.

DOCTOR: It is well known that a man may find many times his strength in the bottle.

ADJUTANT: Mister Drake, this Court will not accept drunkenness as mitigation of any act on the part of Mister Millington.

DRAKE: But does it not, to some extent, reduce his responsibility, Mister President?

ADJUTANT: I do not think so. The responsibility for drinking to excess remains his alone.

DOCTOR: I hardly think, Mister Drake, that this is a line you would do well to pursue.

ADJUTANT: Just so, Doctor.

Against a wall, DRAKE *goes to pick up his notes. He has one point left.* MILLINGTON *noticeably relaxes.* DRAKE *hesitates, uncertain.*

ADJUTANT: Well, Mister Drake. Have you any further questions for this witness?

MILLINGTON: I'd let it drop, if I were you. The cards are against you.

ADJUTANT: Mister Millington. You will not be warned again. Well, Mister Drake, we are waiting.

DRAKE: Doctor. Would you not expect a woman of Mrs Hasseltine's character to be able easily to deal with the importunate advances . . .

ADJUTANT: No. Mister Drake. We are not here to discuss the

character of Mrs Hasseltine, but to judge the actions of Mister Millington.

DRAKE: But it is surely relevant, Mister Preside . . .

ADJUTANT: No. Mister Drake! It is not relevant! You will not refer to the matter again.

DRAKE: . . . But, Mister President. On the very day we arrived here Mister Fothergill issued a warning in the most specific terms, as to the character . . .

ADJUTANT: It is of no concern to this Court what the Junior Subaltern may or may not have chosen to say to you on some private occasion! So far as this Court is concerned Mrs Hasseltine is a woman of the highest character and probity. Do you understand me?

DRAKE: I do not know how I am to defend this officer, if you will allow me no latitude in the matter of . . .

ADJUTANT: You are entitled to whatever 'latitude' I choose to give you as President of this Court and no more! Now. Have I made myself quite plain?

DRAKE: Yes, Mister President, you have indeed.

ADJUTANT: Very well. Confine yourself to questions that are proper to this inquiry.

MILLINGTON: For God's sake, sit down. You're embarrassing us all.

ADJUTANT: Mister Millington, you have interrupted these proceedings for the last time.

DRAKE: Doctor, when Mister Millington passed out at the Mess Night, did you not say that, 'gentlemen who cannot hold their liquor should not drink'?

DOCTOR: . . . I may have said that, yes.

ADJUTANT: I have already told you, Mister Drake.

DRAKE: Well then, surely on the evidence . . . Mister Millington is made not stronger but weaker by alcohol.

DOCTOR: Mister Drake. Since you persist in pursuing this matter, you compel me to tell you, that in my opinion, Mister Millington is on the point of becoming a complete and incurable drunkard. It is almost certain, therefore, that there would be periods when he would have no control whatever over his actions.

Pause.

DRAKE (*to Millington, stunned*): . . . Is this true?

MILLINGTON: Don't sound so shocked, for Christ's sake.

There is a strange, taut, overstrung mixture of amusement, contempt – almost sub-hysteria in Millington at this point.

ADJUTANT: You will not put questions directly to the accused officer, Mister Drake.

MILLINGTON: He has no idea what is required of him, Mister President. You should have made your instructions plainer.

ADJUTANT: Mister Millington . . .

MILLINGTON: You're a fool, Arthur! You are expected to go through the motions, not to indulge a talent for legalistic moralizing!

ADJUTANT: If you continue in this vein, Mister Millington, I shall have you put out at once.

MILLINGTON (*rises*): I should prefer that, Mister President.

ADJUTANT: . . . I have every sympathy with your point of view. You are entitled to rejoin your escort if you wish.

MILLINGTON: Thank you, sir. (*Turns back.*) What a bourgeois little creature you are to be sure, Arthur.

He goes. Pause. Anger directed at Drake.

ADJUTANT: Mister Drake.

DRAKE rises. He is stunned by the attitude of Harper and the Doctor. A reversal that seems to have made him the guilty party. He stands. Silence.

DRAKE (*numbly*): . . . I have no more questions for this witness.

ADJUTANT: Thank you, Mister Drake. (*To Doctor.*) I am sorry if these proceedings have proved distasteful for you, sir. Thank you for attending them.

DOCTOR (*rises*): Mister President. Gentlemen.

The DOCTOR departs. A pause.

ADJUTANT: Mister Fothergill.

JUNIOR SUB (*rises, subdued*): Mister President. The next

logical step would be to call Mrs Hasseltine. I would hope that the defending officer would not find that necessary, but that he would accept a written deposition from her.

ADJUTANT: Exactly so, Mister Fothergill. Mister Drake? (*Pause.*) Mister Drake?

DRAKE: ... I don't know, Mister President. I ... need to think.

ADJUTANT: Very well. This session is now closed, gentlemen. The Court will reconvene at midnight tomorrow. (*He rises.*) You will leave this Mess quickly and quietly, gentlemen. Mister Drake, you will remain here.

They depart, coming to attention: 'Sir.' As Court breaks up LAL *and a* WAITER *surreptitiously appear on veranda from left (seeking Drake). Seeing Adjutant still there, they run off to hide right. Drake and Harper alone. Drake stunned.*

ADJUTANT: Now look here, Drake. What the devil do you think you are playing at?

DRAKE: ... I was trying to do my duty ... as given me by you ... to defend him, sir.

ADJUTANT: To defend him, yes! Not to cast doubts on the persons and institutions of this Regiment!

DRAKE: He is surely entitled to a fair trial?

ADJUTANT: Do you suggest that he will not receive one from us?

DRAKE: I don't know ... what it is that you require of me.

ADJUTANT: You know perfectly well what is required of you. Do not play games with me, sir.

DRAKE: I am to 'go through the motions'. I am to make no serious attempt to defend him.

ADJUTANT: ... There is some doubt in your mind as to his guilt?

DRAKE: No. None whatever ...

ADJUTANT: Very well. Tomorrow you will plead Mister Millington guilty, as clearly he wishes you to. As for yourself, we shall see how you conduct yourself in the weeks to come. You have made an excellent beginning here, Mister

Drake. I should not like to think we have been mistaken in
you, too.

DRAKE: . . . No, sir.

ADJUTANT: Very well. Here is Mrs Hasseltine's deposition.
You will be requiring it since you will not be calling her.
That is all, Mister Drake. (*Starts to go.*)

DRAKE: Mister Harper . . .

ADJUTANT: Well?

DRAKE: Surely Mister Millington is entitled to face his
accuser?

ADJUTANT: Are you being wilfully obstructive, Mister Drake?

DRAKE: No, sir, but . . .

ADJUTANT: Do you not appreciate to what extent we are
already indebted to Mrs Hasseltine? Do you not realize
that, had she made an official charge against him, Mister
Millington would now be facing public court martial. By
officers not of this Regiment? That he would be publicly
disgraced! And so should we!

DRAKE: But is his disgrace not inevitable in any event?

ADJUTANT: Why, Mister Drake?

DRAKE: Well, if he is found guilty, you will surely be obliged
to be rid of him?

ADJUTANT: I do not think so. Mister Millington will find
that we have duties for him yet. Of an unpleasant nature, to
be sure, but admirably well suited to his condition.

DRAKE: You mean to keep him here?

ADJUTANT: For a year or two, certainly, five perhaps, or
even ten. The option lies with us, Mister Drake. We must
see how long it takes Mister Millington to find his place
with us and to learn a simple lesson. That this Regiment is
not mocked.

DRAKE: . . . I see.

ADJUTANT: You can do nothing for Mister Millington and
only harm to yourself. You understand?

DRAKE (*pause: comes to attention*): . . . I request to be relieved of
this duty, sir.

ADJUTANT: No, Mister Drake. You have an admirable
opportunity of serving this Regiment. I shall follow your
progress with the keenest interest. Good night, Mister
Drake.

He goes. DRAKE *stares in an agonizing dilemma. Suddenly
the* WAITER *and* LAL, *an* INDIAN SERVING WOMAN, *re-
appear on the veranda, afraid to be caught.*

WAITER: It is that one, be quick! (*Goes.*)

LAL: Sahib . . . ! Sahib . . . !

DRAKE (*turns*): . . . Yes?

LAL: Ask about the bleeding, sahib!

DRAKE: . . . What?

LAL: The bleeding, sahib. And Mrs Bandanai . . . !

PRADAH SINGH *comes on, furious;* LAL *flees.*

PRADAH: What are you doing here? Be off with you. (*In
Indian.*) Teli chow, Teli chow!

DRAKE: No, wait . . .! (*But she has gone.*)

PRADAH: I am sorry, sahib. It will not happen again, sahib.

DRAKE: . . . Who was that?

PRADAH: The servant of Mem Hasseltine, sahib.

DRAKE: Mrs Hasseltine?

PRADAH: Yes, sahib. I shall take the strongest possible . . .

DRAKE: No. No. (*Pause.*) Pradah Singh, who is Mrs Bandanai?

PRADAH: She is the widow of Jemadar Bandanai, sahib.

DRAKE: Could you . . . arrange for me to speak with her?

PRADAH (*embarrassed*): Well, I . . . I don't know, sahib. It is . . .
not usual, sahib . . .

DRAKE: It is important, Pradah Singh. (*Hesitates.*) It will be of
assistance to Mister Millington.

PRADAH: Millington, sahib?

DRAKE: Whose father I know you greatly admired.

PRADAH: . . . I will see what I can do, sahib.

DRAKE: Thank you, Pradah Singh.

They go.

SCENE THREE

The MESS. *The* TRIAL. *The next midnight.*

DRAKE *enters with papers. He sits in witness chair and begins to write. He has taken a small step to being stronger now. Anger has begun: he has found something that puzzles him.* MILLINGTON *enters.*

MILLINGTON (*very acid, arrogant*): Well. My very own St George. My knight in shining armour. I have come to change my plea, Arthur. Do you understand me? I am changing my plea to guilty.

DRAKE: . . . I understand you very well.

MILLINGTON: Good. (*Pause.*) Well. (*Acid smile.*) No argument as to the honour of the Regiment, Arthur? No insistence on – what was it you called it? – a fair hearing.

DRAKE: You're very confident, aren't you, Millington?

MILLINGTON: I am confident of what I need to be. I must say I regard it as a most unlooked-for blessing if you, too, have been struck by sanity.

DRAKE (*slight pause*): You will not get out of here, Millington. Oh, in a year or two. Five perhaps. Or even ten. Until then we are to be graced with your presence.

MILLINGTON: . . . What are you talking about?

DRAKE: I'm quoting the Adjutant – 'My dear fellow'. They intend to keep you here, Millington. They have duties for you. Of an unpleasant kind.

MILLINGTON: I don't believe you!

DRAKE: Why don't you ask him? The option lies with them.

MILLINGTON: . . . But why? Why?

DRAKE: You are to be taught a lesson, Millington. You are to learn that this Regiment is not mocked.

MILLINGTON: My God. I never thought of that.

DRAKE: No more did I.

HUTTON *comes on.*

HUTTON: Stand up!

Millington now much shaken. The COURT *files on as before. It is clear at once that* JUNIOR SUBALTERN *and* ADJUTANT *are angry with Drake. From their positions they glare at him.*

ADJUTANT: Be seated, gentlemen. (*All sit.*) This Court is now in session.

MILLINGTON (*rises*): Mister President. I must tell you . . .

ADJUTANT: Be silent, Mister Millington!

MILLINGTON: But I . . .

ADJUTANT: If you speak again, I shall have you put out at once. Now sit down, sir.

   MILLINGTON *sits. It has been an automatic gesture of protest. What could he say?*

ADJUTANT: Mister Fothergill.

JUNIOR SUB: Mister President. As you already know – and as I now inform this Court – Mister Drake has this afternoon insisted that Mrs Hasseltine appear before this Court. He will not accept a written deposition from her.

ADJUTANT (*glares at Drake*): I am indeed aware of that, Mister Fothergill.

JUNIOR SUB: I therefore propose to call her now, Mister President.

ADJUTANT: Mister Hutton.

HUTTON: Sir.

DRAKE: But—

ADJUTANT: You have wished to question Mrs Hasseltine, Mister Drake. Very well, now you shall.

DRAKE: But I had no wish to call her yet, Mister President.

ADJUTANT: That is your misfortune, Mister Drake. This Court has not been convened to satisfy your wishes.

HUTTON: Would you come this way, please, ma'am.

ADJUTANT: You will rise, gentlemen.

MRS HASS: Thank you, Mister Hutton.

   They rise as she enters, apparently gracious and calm.

ADJUTANT (*bows*): Ma'am.

MRS HASS: Mister President.

ADJUTANT: I am sorry that we have to disturb you, ma'am. I trust you will appreciate that it is not of our choosing.

MRS HASS: I understand that very well, Mister President. I have, besides, no objection to appearing before this inquiry.

ADJUTANT: Thank you, ma'am. Be seated, please.

MRS HASS: Thank you.

ADJUTANT: Mister Fothergill.

JUNIOR SUB (*goes to her: bows*): Ma'am . . .

MRS HASS: Mister Fothergill . . .

JUNIOR SUB: I should like to ask you just three questions, ma'am. Were you attacked on the night of the seventeenth?

MRS HASS: I was, yes.

JUNIOR SUB: By whom, ma'am?

MRS HASS: By Mister Millington.

JUNIOR SUB: There is no doubt in your mind as to that?

MRS HASS: None whatever. Mister Millington made both his identity and his intentions absolutely plain to me.

JUNIOR SUB: Thank you, ma'am. (*He returns to place.*)

    DRAKE *rises. Recovered from surprise, he proceeds to outmanœuvre them. He is learning guile – and discovering toughness, stubbornness in himself.*

DRAKE: Mister President. I am most anxious to conduct myself in accordance with the requirements laid down by you for this Court. However, it would greatly assist me in . . . presenting a coherent account to this Court . . . if you would permit me to call another witness before I question Mrs Hasseltine.

ADJUTANT: Certainly not, Mister Drake. Mrs Hasseltine has already been greatly inconvenienced, entirely on your account. You will ask your questions now.

DRAKE: . . . With respect, Mister President, I am most anxious not to inconvenience Mrs Hasseltine further. But since I am not yet presenting the case for the defence, I should merely be obliged to recall her at a later date. Whereas this

other matter would take but a moment or two – I do assure
you, ma'am; and you, Mister President.

ADJUTANT: You will not be allowed to recall Mrs Hasseltine
later, Mister Drake.

DRAKE: . . . Again with respect, Mister President, it is my
entitlement – as laid down by you before all the members
of this Court – to call any witness of whatever rank or
station, should I require to do so.

A pause. Harper is trapped by protocol and honour.

ADJUTANT: . . . Whom do you wish to call?

DRAKE: The Second-in-Command, Mister President.

ADJUTANT (*a shock*): . . . Major Roach?

DRAKE: Yes, Mister President.

ADJUTANT: . . . Is he aware of this?

DRAKE: He is waiting in the card room, sir.

ADJUTANT: Very well. (*He is outranked.*) (*Rises.*) I am sorry,
ma'am. It appears that Mister Drake is determined to put
you to the greatest possible inconvenience. I wonder if I
might ask you . . . ?

MRS HASS (*rises*): Of course, Mister President. I am only too
anxious to assist you.

ADJUTANT: Thank you, ma'am.

MRS HASS: Gentlemen . . .

Clearly disturbed, she goes. Harper furious.

ADJUTANT: I am not pleased by this, Mister Drake.

DRAKE: . . . I am sorry, Mister President.

ADJUTANT: Mister Boulton, call the Second-in-Command.

BOULTON *goes off. Silence. Stiffness.* MILLINGTON
murmurs to DRAKE.

MILLINGTON: But why? Why him . . .

ADJUTANT: I've no doubt that if you can contain yourself in
patience, Mister Millington, Mister Drake will enlighten us
all.

BOULTON *returns with* SECOND-IN-COMMAND.

ADJUTANT: Sir.

ROACH: Mister Harper.

ADJUTANT: Be seated, sir, please.

    ROACH *sits: his disapproval of the Court is quite apparent.*
Mister Drake.

DRAKE (*rises*): Sir. Is it a fact that when you sent for me, as defending officer, this morning, you told me that you had witnessed the attack on Mrs Hasseltine by Mister Millington?

ROACH: I did, yes.

    Shock to Court.

DRAKE: In what circumstances, sir?

ROACH: I was Officer of the Week. Mister Hart here was Officer of the Day. At about two o'clock we were just completing our final tour of inspection. I had sent Mister Hart down to look over the native lines. I myself was crossing via the Folly to inspect the perimeter picquet on the Plain.

DRAKE: Yes, sir.

ROACH: As I was passing the Folly, I heard what sounded like some sort of altercation among the shrubbery and trees surrounding it. I stopped. And then I heard Mister Millington's voice. I am not certain as to what he said except that he appeared to be pleading with someone. But then I heard Mrs Hasseltine – very sharply and clearly. She said 'I have already told you, Mister Millington, that I find your advances not only . . . offensive to me, but quite pointless'. Or words very much to that effect.

DRAKE: She must have sounded angry, sir.

ROACH: She did, indeed. Extremely.

DRAKE: And frightened?

ROACH: No. I would have said she sounded – in command of the situation, rather than afraid.

DRAKE: . . . I see. And then, sir?

ROACH: Well, I immediately stepped in among the trees to put an end to this nonsense. But it was extremely dark in there, Mister Drake. In the end I could make them out only from their voices – and then against the paler colour of the stonework.

DRAKE: They were fighting, sir?

ROACH: Mister Millington had hold of Mrs Hasseltine's arm. But before I was able to intervene, she had broken away from him – had ordered him to leave her alone – and had begun to walk angrily back through the trees towards the Mess.

DRAKE: To walk, sir?

ROACH: Yes.

DRAKE: Not to run?

ROACH: No, no. I could see her quite clearly. The lights of the Mess were directly beyond her, if you understand me. About thirty or forty yards away.

DRAKE: Still, she must have appeared extremely distressed.

ROACH: I should have said . . . angry, rather than distressed.

DRAKE: I see. What happened then, sir?

ROACH: Well, you know what happened next, Mister Drake. There was great consternation. The other gentlemen running, myself included. And when I got into the Mess, rather to my surprise, Mrs Hasseltine was indeed in an anguished condition. Extremely so. Far more than I should have imagined.

DRAKE: Why do you say that, sir?

ROACH: Well . . . there is no excuse for Mister Millington's behaviour. None whatever. It was in every sense reprehensible. However, it had not appeared to me to be quite so shocking. Quite so – violent or extreme.

DRAKE: Would it be fair to say, sir, that it was your impression that this was a . . . feeble and unsuccessful attempt on the part of a younger man to force his attentions on an older woman?

ROACH: That would have been my impression, yes. But . . .

ADJUTANT: I must intervene, sir. Exactly what are you trying to establish by this testimony, Mister Drake?

DRAKE: I am merely anxious that the Court should have the clearest possible understanding of what occurred, Mister President.

F

ADJUTANT: I see. But has not the Second-in-Command just given an extremely detailed account of precisely the offence with which Mister Millington is charged? (*To Roach.*) Is that not so, sir?

ROACH: I have, yes. And he should be disciplined for it. (*Angrily.*) But certainly not by an affair of this kind. You know my views in this matter, Mister Harper. The Regiment is ill-served by manifestations of this nature.

ADJUTANT: But would it not be greatly less well served by the alternative, sir?

ROACH: That may be the case. At least it would have the sanction of proper authority behind it.

ADJUTANT: Yes, sir.

ROACH: Very well. I shall express myself – forcibly, gentlemen – at a later date to you all.

ADJUTANT: Sir. Mister Drake.

DRAKE: Finally, sir, I should like to ask you what became of Mister Millington in all of this.

ROACH: I understand from what you have told me, that he was laid out by Mrs Hasseltine. Which is perfectly possible. My view was not clear. Certainly she broke from him with some force. For my own part, I had thought that he had made off into the trees. I had intended to deal with the matter myself, you see. To speak to Mrs Hasseltine, as soon as I returned to the Mess.

DRAKE: But you were overtaken by events?

ROACH: Unhappily, yes, I was.

DRAKE: Thank you, sir. (*He sits.*)

ADJUTANT: . . . I wish to be clear as to exactly what you are saying, sir. You're telling this Court that you witnessed Mister Millington's attack on Mrs Hasseltine?

ROACH: In essence, yes. Though as I say, it was dark.

ADJUTANT: There is no doubt in your mind as to the identity of Mister Millington?

ROACH: None whatever.

ADJUTANT: I see. Then I don't think we need detain you any

further, sir . . . (*Looks at* JUNIOR SUBALTERN *who shakes his head.*) (*Rises.*) Thank you for coming to give evidence before us, sir.

ROACH (*rises*) (*Angry look at them*): Gentlemen . . .

 He goes.

ADJUTANT: Perhaps I should remind you, Mister Drake, that you are here to defend this officer, not to prosecute him. (*General amusement.*)

DRAKE: Thank you, Mister President. In the circumstances of this trial, it as well to be reminded of why we are here.

ADJUTANT: . . . Do you still wish to question Mrs Hasseltine?

DRAKE: Yes, Mister President, I do.

ADJUTANT: Very well. Mister Hutton.

HUTTON: Sir.

 HUTTON *goes off.*

ADJUTANT: I will remind you, Mister Drake, to be courteous.

HUTTON: Will you come in now, please, ma'am.

ADJUTANT (*he rises*): You will rise, gentlemen. (*They rise.*)

 HUTTON *shows* MRS HASSELTINE *on, who is clearly annoyed, cool. (And who is wondering.)*

HUTTON: Ma'am.

ADJUTANT: I am sorry, ma'am. I do not think we shall need to trouble you very much further.

MRS HASS: Very well.

ADJUTANT: Please be seated.

MRS HASS: Thank you . . . (*She sits.*) (*They all sit.*)

 The antipathy between she and Drake is palpable, yet unstated. Drake has remained standing.

DRAKE: Mrs Hasseltine . . .

ADJUTANT: Before Mister Drake begins to question you, ma'am, I should tell you that the Second-in-Command has just informed this Court that he witnessed Mister Millington's attack on you.

MRS HASS: . . . I see. Thank you.

DRAKE: Mrs Hasseltine, the Second-in-Command has indeed

made it perfectly plain that Mister Millington's behaviour
was totally improper.

MRS HASS: It was indeed.

DRAKE: It must have been . . . very frightening for you,
ma'am.

MRS HASS: It is hardly agreeable to be attacked in the darkness, Mister Drake.

ADJUTANT: Just so, Mister Drake.

DRAKE: Particularly in so isolated a spot.

MRS HASS: As you say.

DRAKE: I am wondering how you came to be there, ma'am?

MRS HASS (*smiles*): There is no mystery as to that, Mister
Drake. There is a stone bench there. You may not have been
with us long enough yet to have discovered it.

DRAKE (*smiles*): I discovered it this afternoon, ma'am. Indeed
I sampled it. You cannot have found it more comfortable.
Perhaps more convenient than a seat here, in the Mess?

MRS HASS: Were you a woman, Mister Drake, you would
understand that – even at the most enjoyable Ball; where
one is outnumbered – there are moments when one wishes
to be alone.

DRAKE: Just so, ma'am. And it was here, at the bench, that
Mister Millington . . . disturbed you?

MRS HASS: He did, yes.

DRAKE: He . . . sprang out at you?

MRS HASS: Hardly that, Mister Drake.

DRAKE: He spoke to you?

MRS HASS: . . . Yes.

DRAKE: In, forgive me, an improper manner?

MRS HASS: . . . Yes.

DRAKE: And you . . . rose at once to leave? You called out?

MRS HASS: Not at once, no.

DRAKE: You did not think it necessary, ma'am?

MRS HASS: I did not, at once, realize how drunk nor how
determined he was.

DRAKE: I see. You did not wish to get him into trouble?

MRS HASS: No. Not then. I thought he was just being stupid.

DRAKE: But he persisted.

MRS HASS: He did indeed. He made it quite plain why he was doing so.

DRAKE: Well, forgive me, ma'am. But you are an extremely attractive woman. You must have found yourself having to deal with silly young gentlemen before this?

ADJUTANT: Mister Drake, it is of no concern to this Court what may have happened in the past.

DRAKE: It was intended purely as a general observation, Mister President.

MRS HASS: I am not accustomed to dealing with young men who are determinedly and viciously drunk, Mister Drake.

DRAKE: ... Viciously drunk, ma'am?

MRS HASS: Mister Millington made it absolutely plain that he was determined to use me as a means of having himself dismissed from this Regiment.

DRAKE: I see. And so you were compelled to fight him?

MRS HASS: ... I was, yes.

DRAKE: To hit him?

MRS HASS: Yes.

DRAKE: With what, ma'am?

MRS HASS: ... My fists ... my arms. Whatever came to hand.

DRAKE: And did anything come to hand, ma'am?

MRS HASS: I don't understand you, Mister Drake.

DRAKE: You struck him with your fan perhaps?

MRS HASS: I must have done, yes.

DRAKE: Or your bag?

MRS HASS: I imagine so.

DRAKE: Were you carrying anything else?

MRS HASS: No, why?

DRAKE: Did you perhaps pick up a stone?

MRS HASS: ... I don't think so, no.

DRAKE: Or a fallen branch?

ADJUTANT: I think, ma'am, that Mister Drake is referring to ...

DRAKE: I am referring to the injury sustained by Mister Millington, ma'am. There is a gash – an extremely unpleasant gash, about two inches long – behind his ear.

MRS HASS: Well, that's right – yes. I do remember now that I struck at him. With my arm. Like that. (*Demonstrates downward blow.*)

DRAKE: With your right arm?

MRS HASS: Yes. Well . . . yes, I think so . . .

DRAKE: Are you right-handed, Mrs Hasseltine?

MRS HASS: . . . Yes, I am.

DRAKE (*dryly: convinced now she lies*): Were you standing behind him at the time, ma'am?

MRS HASS: . . . I'm afraid I don't . . .

DRAKE: The injury is to the right-hand side of his head, Mrs Hasseltine.

MRS HASS: . . . Well, really, Mister Drake! We were fighting. In the darkness. I really cannot be expected . . .

ADJUTANT: Exactly so, Mister Drake. You are asking the witness to remember events that happened at a time of great stress for her.

MRS HASS: Just so, Mister President.

DRAKE (*quickly*): I am sorry, ma'am. Forgive me. It is quite unreasonable of me to expect you to remember details of that kind.

ADJUTANT: . . . Very well, Mister Drake.

DRAKE: We may take it, however, that you did hit him?

ADJUTANT: We have already taken that, Mister Drake.

MRS HASS: . . . I did, yes.

DRAKE (*very clearly*): With what, ma'am?

MRS HASS: Perhaps it was a stone, as you say . . .

DRAKE: I do not think so, ma'am.

ADJUTANT: Mister Drake . . .

DRAKE: I searched the Folly for over three hours this afternoon, ma'am. I found no vestige of one for over a hundred yards in any direction.

MRS HASS: Then it must have been a branch—

DRAKE: There is nothing, Mrs Hasseltine. Not a stick. Not a stone. Nothing with which you could possibly have struck Mister Millington. Nothing that could be lifted by a dozen men, let alone one woman.

MRS HASS: Really this is too absurd!

ADJUTANT: It is surely not beyond your powers of imagination, Mister Drake, to realize that Mister Millington probably fell back against a tree, or against a wall, when Mrs Hasseltine broke away from him.

MRS HASS: Exactly so, Mister President . . .

MILLINGTON: I was hit, Mister President!

ADJUTANT: Be silent, sir.

MILLINGTON ⎤ : She hit me! (*Completely baffled.*)
DRAKE ⎬ : Be quiet!
ADJUTANT ⎦ : Will you be quiet, sir!

MRS HASS: Of course, if you prefer to take the word of the accused officer against that of myself . . .

ADJUTANT: Certainly not, ma'am. That does not arise. Mister Drake, this has gone far enough.

DRAKE (*hurriedly*): I am sorry, Mister President . . .

ADJUTANT: You will end your questions now.

DRAKE: But I only have a question or two more, Mister President – and I readily accept that this was a misunderstanding on my part. I see now that Mister Millington probably fell back against this wall, or tree, ma'am, and that you escaped from him. And that you ran screaming a matter of forty yards or so to the Mess.

ADJUTANT: Mister Drake. We have already had the evidence of the Second-in-Command that in the first instance . . .

DRAKE: Of course, Mister President. I am sorry. In the first instance you walked, ma'am. (*Slight pause.*) And then perhaps you ran? Perhaps you feared he might attack you again?

MRS HASS: That thought did enter my mind, yes.

DRAKE: He didn't, of course, ma'am?

MRS HASS: No, Mister Drake. He did not.

DRAKE: Then he must have attacked you with extreme severity on the first occasion. Exactly what did he do, ma'am?

MRS HASS: Well, he . . .

DRAKE: Did he take hold of your arm?

MRS HASS: He did, yes.

DRAKE: And he pulled you about?

MRS HASS: Yes.

DRAKE: And then, ma'am?

MRS HASS: Well, he . . .

DRAKE: Yes, ma'am?

MRS HASS: . . . Really, I cannot be expected to remember —

DRAKE: Well, did he perhaps attempt to place his hand on your bosom? Your dress was torn—

ADJUTANT: Mister Drake—

MRS HASS: He may have done, yes.

DRAKE: Well, did he, or didn't he, ma'am?

MRS HASS: I can't remember, Mister Drake!

DRAKE: But this was a terrifying experience for you, Mrs Hasseltine. You ran, screaming, all the way into the Mess!

MRS HASS (*rises: blazing*): Exactly what are you implying?

ADJUTANT (*jumps up*): That is all, Mister Drake! Sit down!

DRAKE: I have only one more question for this . . .

ADJUTANT: No, Mister Drake! Be seated!

　　Pause.

DRAKE: Why are you lying, Mrs Hasseltine?

ADJUTANT: Mister Drake!

MRS HASS: How dare you! How dare you, Mister Drake!

ADJUTANT: Ma'am, if you will allow me to . . .

MRS HASS (*storming out*): I shall tolerate no more of this, Mister President! You may play your childish games in future without me!

　　She is gone. A shocked silence. Millington dazed, baffled. In silence the ADJUTANT *comes round the table.*

ADJUTANT: You have finished yourself here, Mister Drake. Do you hear me. You are finished here.

DRAKE (*sick at heart*): If what I have heard in this courtroom is typical of the honour of this Regiment . . . then I shall be only too happy to depart.

ADJUTANT: And we shall be only too happy to accommodate you. Now the rest of you, pay attention to me . . .

DRAKE: That woman is lying, Mister Harper.

ADJUTANT: Be silent, sir! (*Pause.*) This Court will reconvene at midnight tomorrow, when this matter will be ended. You hear me, Mister Drake? Ended.

DRAKE (*pause: nods slowly*): . . . Yes, Mister President.

ADJUTANT: Very well. That is all.

He stalks out. Pause, the others leave. Drake, Millington alone. Drake is near to tears, but for him this is not possible. Millington has no way to express sympathy for this man. Pause.

DRAKE: . . . I thought this was a Regiment of honour.

MILLINGTON (*embarrassed*): So it is, my dear fellow. A Regiment of the highest honour. As you yourself have made plain to me.

DRAKE: It appears that I owe you an apology, Mister Millington.

MILLINGTON: What's going on, Arthur?

DRAKE: I do not know.

MILLINGTON: Why should she lie?

DRAKE: . . . It may be that she is not.

MILLINGTON: But she fetched me the devil of a crack.

DRAKE: . . . Why don't you go to bed?

MILLINGTON: Why not?

Starts to go, turns back. In his own way flippant, awkward, tries to help.

Look here, Arthur, if you wish to remain here . . . you really will have to abandon this enterprise. It isn't too late.

DRAKE: I fancy I can survive without your sympathy, Millington. Yours least of all.

MILLINGTON: You disappoint me, Arthur. Is it just pride then? Wounded pride?

DRAKE: . . . Let us call it principle. Why not? 'Bourgeois'

principle. But that, of course, is something that you would not understand.

MILLINGTON: No, that is true. I am told, though, that it is invincible.

DRAKE: Are you? Well. Then you have met . . . an invincible man, have you not?

MILLINGTON: . . . Good night, Arthur.

> *Goes quickly. Pause. At last* DRAKE *covers his face in pain. A grunt comes from him.*

DRAKE: Oh, God!

> PRADAH SINGH *comes urgently on.*

PRADAH: Sahib . . . ! Sahib . . . !

DRAKE: Yes . . . ?

PRADAH: Mrs Bandanai is here.

DRAKE (*absorbed: almost indifferent*): Ah . . . Yes. Thank you, Pradah Singh . . .

PRADAH: She was attacked too, sahib.

DRAKE (*becoming alert*): Attacked?

PRADAH: Yes, sahib.

DRAKE: When?

PRADAH: I do not know, but . . .

DRAKE: Where is she?

PRADAH: She is outside.

DRAKE (*briskly, turning away*): Bring her in.

PRADAH: In here, sahib, it is improper . . .

DRAKE: Bring her in, Pradah Singh! That's an order.

PRADAH: . . . Sahib.

> *Unwilling* PRADAH SINGH *goes.* DRAKE *paces, impatient.* PRADAH SINGH *returns steering* MRS BANDANAI. *She is withdrawn, unwilling, hides face.* PRADAH SINGH *disapproves of, resists what follows.*

PRADAH: Ja ha! Ja ha!

> This is Mrs Bandanai, sahib.

DRAKE: Sit down, ma'am, please.

PRADAH: Bato. Bato.

DRAKE: . . . Doesn't she speak English?

PRADAH: No, sahib. (*Pause.*) She does not wish to speak at all, sahib.

DRAKE: Well . . . tell her I mean her no harm.

PRADAH: Ushi kutch apsi uprad nahi.

DRAKE: Tell her, there is a young officer in trouble . . .

PRADAH: Ik offcer takflifna ha.

DRAKE: That I wish to help him . . .

PRADAH: Ushi sahib madat kema chahati ha . . .

DRAKE: But without her I cannot.

PRADAH: Upki sewa madat nehi osata.

MRS BANDANAI: Engarasi suar ko main kum madat marun, una merna do, muja keya parya.

PRADAH: Bas! Bas!

DRAKE: What did she say?

PRADAH: . . . She is overwrought, sahib. (*To Mrs Bandanai.*) Asamat bolo' . . .

DRAKE: No. Tell me what she said.

PRADAH: Very well. She said 'Why should I help the English pig, let him die, I don't care.'

DRAKE: Ask her if it is true she was attacked.

PRADAH: Kaya such hai apako kesina hath lagaya?

MRS BANDANAI: Je hain such hai.

PRADAH: It is true, sahib.

DRAKE: When?

PRADAH: . . . Sahib, I . . .

DRAKE: Ask her when.

PRADAH: Kabi?

MRS BANDANAI: Cha mana pahla.

PRADAH: Jut! Jut!

MRS BANDANAI: Nahin, nahin, main jut nahin bolte!

DRAKE: What does she say, Pradah Singh?

PRADAH: . . . She says – six months ago, sahib.

DRAKE: Six months! Ask her who, Pradah Singh.

PRADAH: . . . Sahib . . . I cannot.

DRAKE: Ask her who.

PRADAH: Kuan tha?

MRS BANDANAI: Nahin bataguin! Nahin bataguin!

PRADAH: She will not tell you, sahib.

DRAKE: Ask her what happened, then.

PRADAH: I am not in a position . . .

DRAKE: Ask her!

PRADAH: Keya huwa.

    MRS BANDANAI *begins her halting story which* PRADAH SINGH *translates.*

MRS BANDANAI: Main ek offcer ke sath thee, uska sath suithee, ekali thee, wa bungla chor ka chalagaya.

PRADAH: . . . She was with an officer. She had been with him . . . lain with him, sahib. She was alone, he had left the bungalow.

MRS BANDANAI: Nagi thee, char payee ke upar.

PRADAH: She was naked, sahib. On the bed.

MRS BANDANAI: Ethna mai ek admi aya, gera lal aur suana ke tera.

PRADAH: There came another man, she said, another man in scarlet and gold . . .

MRS BANDANAI: Unena muja kaha char payee sa utho, hath aur paun sa duro.

PRADAH: He made her – get off the bed, sahib. He made her run about . . . naked . . . on her hands and knees . . .

MRS BANDANAI: Aur suar ke tera awaz be bano. Eska pas telwar be thee.

PRADAH: She had to make noises, noises like a . . . He had a sword.

DRAKE: . . . You don't . . . ?

PRADAH: . . . It is the game. It is the game as they play it in the Mess. Sticking the pig. With a sword. From behind. As it runs . . .

DRAKE: Oh, my God . . . No . . .

    DRAKE *shocked, sickened.* PRADAH SINGH *comforts the murmuring* MRS BANDANAI.

PRADAH: It is the game, sahib. I am certain.

MRS BANDANAI: Bahutu buri bath hui, bahutu buri bath hui.

PRADAH: Theke hai, theke hai . . .

DRAKE: . . . But who? . . . Who could do such a thing . . .?

PRADAH: Nam bola?

MRS BANDANAI: Engaras . . .

PRADAH: An Englishman, sahib.

DRAKE: Who? Ask her who, Pradah Singh! Tell her I must
know! Tell her that I will find this man! That I will stop
him! That I will not cover up the truth!

PRADAH: Nam botal . . .

MRS BANDANAI: Main nahin bata sakti, muja yanhan sa
pension melta hai, nai kesi par dosh nahn laga sakti.

PRADAH: . . . She cannot tell you, sahib. She has a pension
from this Regiment: how can she accuse an . . .

DRAKE: A pension! For God's sake! This is my life! (*Seizes
Mrs Bandanai*.) This is my life!

She looks up. It seems that she understands.

MRS BANDANAI: Scarlett.

She jumps up and makes for the veranda.

MRS BANDANAI: Captain Scarlett . . . !

PRADAH: Jut! Jut!

MRS BANDANAI: Main such bolti huin . . . Captain Scarlett
. . . (*She runs off.*)

PRADAH: Wapas auo wapas auo . . .

DRAKE: Captain Scarlett . . . ?

PRADAH: Yes, sahib.

DRAKE: . . . But . . .

PRADAH: He was killed in the Mutiny, sahib.

DRAKE: He's dead!

Slight pause.

PRADAH: Yes, sahib. Captain Scarlett – is dead.

DRAKE (*stunned: afraid*): . . . What . . . What's happening . . . ?

CURTAIN

ACT THREE

SCENE ONE

The MESS. *The Trial. The next Midnight.*

MILLINGTON *is waiting, clearly worried.* DRAKE *enters carrying a wrapped parcel which he places on Defence table.*

MILLINGTON: Arthur, I must . . . speak with you—

DRAKE: And I, you—

MILLINGTON: I have been thinking, my dear fellow and, ah—

DRAKE: I know now that you spoke the truth, Millington.

MILLINGTON: . . . What?

DRAKE: You may have been stupid, but you were not vicious.

MILLINGTON: No . . . Besides I rather like her as a matter of fact . . .

DRAKE: . . . Look here. I want you to trust me, Millington. Tonight's proceedings will not be pleasant, but you must remain quiet whatever happens . . .

MILLINGTON: That is what I wanted to speak to you about . . .

DRAKE: . . . What?

MILLINGTON: Look here, Arthur, I went riding this morning . . .

DRAKE: I'm afraid I don't . . .

MILLINGTON: No. No, let me finish, please . . . I received this note from the Colonel. Yes. 'The Colonel presents his compliments to Mister Millington, and wonders whether Mister Millington might care to exercise the Colonel's string again. The Colonel would of course be grateful if Mister Millington would endeavour to maintain contact with the Colonel's animals on this occasion.' I like horses, Arthur . . .

DRAKE: Millington.

MILLINGTON: It is in one, do you see, Arthur. One is not to escape. I felt this morning as you must . . . That one is intended for a particular place. So you see, Arthur, you are destroying yourself here for no reason . . . I . . .

DRAKE: You are not to concern yourself with me.

MILLINGTON: But I do, Arthur. I know what this place means to you.

DRAKE: No. No. I do not expect to remain here.

HUTTON: Come to order.

The COURT *files on and all stand behind their chairs.*

ADJUTANT: Before I convene this Court, I am told, Mister Drake, that you have recalled the Doctor.

DRAKE: Yes, Mister President, I have.

ADJUTANT: I told you this matter would be ended tonight, and it will be!

DRAKE: So it will, Mister President – that I guarantee.

ADJUTANT: Very well. Be seated, gentlemen.

They all do so.

This Court is now in session. Mister Fothergill?

JUNIOR SUB (*rises*): I have no more witnesses to call, Mister President. I have here written depositions from the Colonel, Major Wimbourne, Major Forster of the Lancers, and Mrs Forster. (*Acid smile.*) I presume, of course, that Mister Drake will accept them.

ADJUTANT: Quite so. Mister Drake?

DRAKE (*rises*): With pleasure, Mister President.

ADJUTANT (*nods to Fothergill*): Very well.

JUNIOR SUBALTERN *crosses, puts one before Adjutant.*

JUNIOR SUB: Mister President.

Crosses, hands second group of sheets to DRAKE.

DRAKE: Thank you. (*Puts depositions disinterestedly to one side.*)

JUNIOR SUB: The case for the prosecution is now closed, Mister President.

ADJUTANT: Thank you, Mister Fothergill.

JUNIOR SUBALTERN *sits.*

Mister Drake.

DRAKE: I call the Doctor, Mister President.

ADJUTANT: Mister Hutton.

    HUTTON *goes to entrance and ushers* DOCTOR *in.*

HUTTON: Sir . . . Would you come in please, Doctor.

DOCTOR (*nervous*): Thank you, thank you. (*Bows to* ADJUTANT.)

ADJUTANT: I am sorry that we should have had to recall you, Doctor.

DOCTOR: So am I, Mister President, so am I, but no matter.

ADJUTANT (*indicates chair*): Sir . . .

    DOCTOR *sits.*

  Mister Drake.

DRAKE (*rises*): Doctor. Two nights ago I questioned you as to the injuries sustained by Mrs Hasseltine.

DOCTOR: You did, yes.

DRAKE: Why did you not tell us, Doctor, that she had been attacked with a sword?

DOCTOR: . . . With a sword?

MILLINGTON: A sword . . . ?

ADJUTANT: Be quiet, Mister Millington. What is this about, Mister Drake?

DRAKE: Mister President. I am prepared to substantiate every single statement that I make tonight, however unpleasant, with facts. I take it you will accept factual evidence, Mister President.

DOCTOR (*bewildered*): I do not know how you can prove she was attacked with a sword, Mister Drake—

DRAKE: Then you will have no objection to my trying, sir?

DOCTOR: None whatever . . .

MILLINGTON (*rising*): But I had no sword!

DRAKE: Trust me! Mister President?

ADJUTANT: Very well.

DRAKE: Doctor. Does the name Bandanai mean anything to you? Mrs Bandanai?

DOCTOR: . . . It does, yes.

DRAKE: Have you recently had occasion to examine her?

DOCTOR: . . . Yes, I have.

DRAKE: Why, Doctor, because she had been attacked?

DOCTOR: She had been, yes. But—

DRAKE: In what manner, Doctor?

DOCTOR: I cannot answer a question of that kind. It requires a breach of medical ethics.

DRAKE: Then allow me to make it easy for you, Doctor. She was attacked with a sword, was she not?

DOCTOR: It is possible.

DRAKE: Possible? Very well. Let me re-phrase my question. She was attacked with a blade, was she not?

DOCTOR: . . . She was, yes – but as I have already said . . .

DRAKE: Are you familiar with the expression 'making a point', Doctor?

DOCTOR: Naturally I am – yes.

DRAKE: What does it mean?

DOCTOR: It refers to a game that is played in the Mess.

DRAKE: What sort of game?

DOCTOR: The – pursuit of a stuffed pig, or boar.

DRAKE: And what is the object of this game?

DOCTOR: To – pierce the – animal with the point of a sword.

DRAKE: Where, Doctor?

DOCTOR: It is simply to make a hit. I don't think it matters where.

DRAKE: Is it not the object of the exercise to pierce that part of the anatomy which is presented in flight – that is to say, the hindquarters?

DOCTOR: It is simply an effigy after all, Mister Drake.

DRAKE: Well, where did this game originate, Doctor – in the field?

DOCTOR: I imagine so.

DRAKE: And are those effigies, or living animals?

DOCTOR: But it is – a well-known sport, Mister Drake. It is played all over . . .

DRAKE: What is a sport, Doctor? To penetrate the anus of a living animal with steel?

G

DOCTOR: That is a revolting suggestion!

DRAKE: It is a revolting game – but that is the Regimental variation, is it not?

ADJUTANT: No, Mister Drake! You will not—

DRAKE: Mister President! Would you care to ask the Doctor where Mrs Bandanai sustained her injuries?!

DOCTOR: You . . . are not . . . ?

DRAKE: I am saying nothing, Doctor, which I do not know and cannot prove to be a fact.

ADJUTANT: Mister Drake . . .

DRAKE: I am saying, Mister President, that somebody played the Regimental game . . . with Mrs Bandanai in the role of pig.

DOCTOR: That is a horrible idea . . .

DRAKE: Yes, Doctor, it is. But were the injuries not consistent with precisely that form of attack?

> DOCTOR *horrified, he cannot answer.*

ADJUTANT: The Court requires an answer to that question, Doctor.

DOCTOR: They would be consistent, yes, but . . .

DRAKE: Thank you, Doctor.

DOCTOR: But it never entered my head . . .

> DRAKE *has returned to Defence table and is unwrapping parcel.*

DRAKE: Now, Doctor, three days ago you examined Mrs Hasseltine?

> DRAKE *has the dress by the shoulders, his back to the Doctor.*

DOCTOR: There is no connection between the two cases.

DRAKE: None, Doctor?

DOCTOR: Surely not?

> DRAKE *turns with the dress.*

DRAKE: Do you know what this is?

DOCTOR: It's Mrs Hasseltine's dress.

DRAKE: Yes, Doctor. The one she was wearing on the night she was attacked. I got it from the hospital. The Indian woman who was told to burn it thought it too valuable and kept it instead. You see that the skirt is soaked in blood?

DOCTOR: Well, she was cut.

DRAKE: Where, Doctor?

DOCTOR: On the thigh.

DRAKE: High up on the thigh?

DOCTOR: On the thigh, Mister Drake.

DRAKE: Not on the buttock?

DOCTOR: I have already said ...

DRAKE (*showing skirt*): About there?

DOCTOR: Well, yes.

DRAKE: How would you describe that, Doctor?

DOCTOR: It looks like a tear ...

DRAKE: A tear? It has absolutely straight, uniform sides, has it not? Is it not a cut – such as might be made by a blade in piercing the material?

DOCTOR: ... Really, I cannot say.

DRAKE: Doctor ...

ADJUTANT: Let me see the dress.

DRAKE: Yes, Mister President ... (*Hands him the dress.*)

MILLINGTON (*rises*): But I didn't attack her with a sword!

DRAKE: Nobody is suggesting that you did.

    ADJUTANT *looks at Drake ... Then at Millington.*

ADJUTANT (*quieter, but firm*): Sit down, sir.

    MILLINGTON *sits.*

    ADJUTANT *examines cut for some moments. This is a turning point for him – as Drake recognizes.*

There is no question, Doctor, but that this was made with a sword.

DOCTOR: I examined the woman, not her clothing. I had no reason to suppose ...

DRAKE: Well, now that you have reason to suppose, let me ask you, whether the injuries in both cases suggest attempts at the same form of attack, by the same man?

DOCTOR: But – Mrs Hasseltine – identified her attacker!

DRAKE: And Mrs Bandanai did not?

DOCTOR: No. No, she didn't.

DRAKE: She has now, Doctor. Now she has. Do you still believe that these two were isolated and unconnected attacks?

DOCTOR: No, I would now think . . . that it is quite possible they were not.

DRAKE: Thank you, Doctor.

DOCTOR: But it never entered my head. I had no reason to doubt Mrs Hasseltine's word.

DRAKE: I know that, Doctor. Now, when did you examine Mrs Bandanai?

DOCTOR: . . . About six months ago.

DRAKE: Six months?

DOCTOR: Yes.

DRAKE: You appreciate, of course, that Mister Millington was not here six months ago?

DOCTOR: I do.

DRAKE: So that if these attacks were the work of the same man, it could not have been Mister Millington?

DOCTOR: I realize that now.

DRAKE: Thank you, Doctor.

ADJUTANT: Mister Drake . . .

DRAKE: Mister President. It is my belief that on the night of the seventeenth, Mrs Hasseltine was attacked not once, but twice. On the first occasion – if his pathetic attempt to make advances to her can be called an assault – by Mister Millington. And on the second occasion – after he had struck Mister Millington unconscious with the hilt of his sword – by another man. With that same sword.

ADJUTANT: . . . Who?

DRAKE: Perhaps the Doctor can help us. How did Mrs Bandanai come to the hospital, Doctor? Was she brought?

DOCTOR: She was, yes.

DRAKE: By whom? An officer of this Regiment?

DOCTOR: I don't believe I am required to answer that question.

ADJUTANT: The Court instructs you to, Doctor.

DOCTOR: Very well – yes she was.

DRAKE: By an officer of this Regiment.

DOCTOR: Yes.

DRAKE: Are you prepared to say whom?

DOCTOR (*rises*): No.

ADJUTANT (*rises*): Doctor ...

DOCTOR: No, Mister Harper. You have already far exceeded the limitations of your inquiry into this matter. I shall asnwer no further questions.

Departs angry. The ADJUTANT *stands, deeply shaken. Looks at dress. Slowly sits.*

ADJUTANT: The Doctor is right, Mister Drake.

DRAKE: Mister President. Before you inform the Colonel, as I realize you must, I should be grateful if you would allow me to call the Second-in-Command, who is waiting to give evidence.

ADJUTANT: ... He has ... knowledge of this matter?

DRAKE: He was the last person to see Mrs Hasseltine before she was attacked.

ADJUTANT (*pause: nods*): ... Very well.

DRAKE: Thank you, Mister President.

ADJUTANT: Mister Hutton.

HUTTON: Sir.

They all look changed now, subdued, uncertain.

DRAKE: Mister President. In questioning the Second-in-Command, I shall have to begin with a matter which may appear irrelevant to this Court. I should be grateful if you would bear with me.

ADJUTANT *nods.* HUTTON *ushers in* ROACH.

HUTTON: Would you come this way please, sir.

ADJUTANT: Good evening, sir. Please be seated.

ROACH: Very well. (*He sits.*)

ADJUTANT: Mister Drake.

DRAKE: Sir. I should like to ask you about Captain Scarlett.

ROACH (*indicates with head*): John Scarlett, do you mean?

DRAKE: The officer whose tunic is in that case, yes, sir.

ROACH: What about him, Mister Drake?

DRAKE: How did he die, sir?

ROACH: That is surely a well-known part of the Regiment's history?

DRAKE: I'm afraid I cannot exactly remember the details, sir.

ROACH: Well, you should, Mister Drake, you should.

DRAKE: Yes, sir.

ROACH: Mm. Well . . . John Scarlett, Major Wimbourne and I were subalterns together. At the Battle of Ratjahpur, John and I were taken prisoner. When he heard about it, Major Wimbourne got together a team of volunteers to attempt a rescue. He did not know that they were holding John and me separately, some two or three hundred yards apart. It so happened that he came to the place where they were holding me, first, and we were able to break out of the Rebel position. But when we went on down the line to rescue John, we were too late. He was already dead.

DRAKE: . . . How exactly had he died, sir?

ROACH: He was flayed, Mister Drake. Flayed alive.

DRAKE: . . . I see.

ROACH: Not a particularly agreeable spectacle.

DRAKE: . . . But he was . . . recognizable, sir?

ROACH: Well, the face was . . . terribly distorted, of course. Flaying involves the . . . removal of the skin – as you probably know.

DRAKE: Yes, sir.

ROACH: And then, too, the . . . body had been mutilated. The . . . eyes and tongue had been put out. The . . . sex removed —

DRAKE: But it had been . . . Captain John Scarlett?

ROACH: Oh. Yes. No question of that whatever.

DRAKE: You saw him with your own eyes, sir?

ROACH: Oh, yes I saw him.

ADJUTANT: Mister Drake.

DRAKE: Yes, Mister President. (*To Roach*.) I am sorry, sir.

ROACH: . . . What? That's all right, Mister Drake. Though I am bound to say I cannot see how . . .

DRAKE: I'd like to return now to the night of the seventeenth, sir. (*Picks up notes.*) You have stated that you saw Mrs Hasseltine with Mister Millington in the Folly, and that she broke away from him and began to walk, back through the trees, towards the Mess?

ROACH: That's right, yes.

DRAKE: What happened then, sir?

ROACH: Well, you know what happened next, Mister Drake.

DRAKE: No, I mean to say, between the time that she walked away, and when she screamed.

ROACH (*puzzled*): I don't believe that anything happened, Mister Drake.

DRAKE: Well, what did you do, sir?

ROACH: Oh, I see. Well I was anxious to inspect the perimeter picquet, as I told you. They'd been extremely sloppy on the first occasion. It often happens on Ball nights . . .

DRAKE: You went across to inspect them, sir?

ROACH: I did, yes. I'd just about reached them, as far as I can remember . . . Yes, I had, I'd just reached them when the outcry occurred.

DRAKE: You didn't by chance have Mrs Hasseltine in view at that moment, did you, sir?

ROACH: No, well as I said, I hadn't considered the incident sufficiently grave actually to follow her.

DRAKE: What did you do then, sir?

ROACH: I ran towards the Mess.

DRAKE: While you were running, sir, did you see anyone in among the trees or emerging from the trees, even?

ROACH: . . . I don't think so . . . Major Wimbourne ran past me . . .

DRAKE: Major Wimbourne, sir?

ROACH: Yes . . . and Mister Boulton and Mister Winters . . .

DRAKE: Did anyone seem to come from the direction of the trees? Not from the Plain, but from your right?

ROACH: I don't think so, Mister Drake, no . . . Yet curiously enough . . .

DRAKE: Yes, sir?

ROACH: No, no, it's too absurd . . .

DRAKE: . . . Well, what is it, sir? It may be important.

ROACH: That I doubt. It's simply that . . . when I first went into the trees – when I heard them speaking together . . . I had the curious impression that . . . that I was not alone. That I was being . . . watched by someone else.

DRAKE: . . . By another man, do you mean, sir?

ROACH: It's ridiculous, of course. It often happens at night. You've no idea how many shots are discharged at shadows, Mister Drake.

DRAKE: Yes, sir – but . . . you did get that impression, sir?

ROACH: For a moment yes . . . Quite strongly, as a matter of fact.

DRAKE (*carefully*): You've no idea . . . Who it was, sir?

ROACH (*smiles*): It was no one, Mister Drake. It was a shadow, as I say. I shouldn't have mentioned it, but you happened to ask that particular question.

DRAKE: But you see, sir, it has been established that Mrs Hasseltine was attacked for a second time that night—

ROACH: For a second time?

DRAKE: Yes, sir. Violently attacked.

ROACH: By Mister Millington, do you mean?

DRAKE: No, sir. By somebody else.

ROACH: By somebody else . . .

DRAKE: Yes, sir.

ROACH (*real distress for his beloved Regiment. Rises*): Are you sure of this?

DRAKE: I can prove it, sir.

ROACH: But . . . by whom, Mister Drake?

DRAKE: That has yet to be established, sir.

ROACH (*turns: goes up*): Has the Colonel been informed of this, Mister Harper?

ADJUTANT: I was about to tell him, sir.

ROACH (*strongly*): You most certainly should, at once!

COLONEL *enters the Mess. Shock.*

ADJUTANT: Colonel!

ALL *rise. Pause.* COLONEL *comes forward and looks slowly round.*

COLONEL: Gentlemen, I enter this Mess – my own Mess – and find a trial in progress, involving my junior officers, that has gone so far beyond the bounds of reasonable authority in this matter, as to strike at the very heart and centre of this Regiment. You do not need to be told that I am displeased. Displeased and gravely disappointed. If there is one quality above all others that is the very mark of an officer – and of a gentleman – it is loyalty. Do you understand me, gentlemen? Loyalty.

Murmurs of assent – 'Colonel . . . Colonel.'

Very well. You will now return to your quarters. Silently and at once. You, Mister Harper, will remain here.

ADJUTANT: Colonel.

COLONEL: So will you, Mister Drake.

DRAKE: Colonel.

COLONEL: The rest of you will report to me, in this Mess, at eight a.m. tomorrow morning. That is all.

THEY *go, coming to attention 'Colonel'. The* **Court** *evaporates . . .*

Would you be good enough to wait in my office, Lionel. I shall require to speak to you after this.

ROACH: Yes, of course, Colonel.

He goes. A pause.

COLONEL: We shall return to your part in this affair in the morning, Mister Harper.

ADJUTANT: Colonel.

COLONEL: I am told, Mister Drake, that you have made an allegation in this room tonight, so . . . gross in detail, so insulting in its implication, that I can hardly believe that I have heard the Doctor correctly.

DRAKE: Colonel—

COLONEL: Be silent, sir. You have been permitted to come to a Regiment of the very highest honour and integrity, Mister Drake. A Regiment whose history and traditions stretch far back into the past – far beyond the life-span of any single man . . . And you have chosen to repay this privilege with an insult so . . . intolerable, so . . .wounding—

DRAKE: Permission to speak, Colonel—

COLONEL: No, sir! You have nothing to say to me. I am barely able to bring myself to speak to you.

DRAKE: But these are facts, Colonel, which I can prove to be true.

COLONEL: You cannot prove an impossibility.

DRAKE: I am sorry, Colonel, but—

COLONEL: No, sir! There is – no officer in this Regiment – capable of what you have suggested.

The COLONEL is struggling to reject something which strikes at the basic premise of his entire life.

ADJUTANT: Colonel . . .

COLONEL: No, sir!

DRAKE: I beg you to ask the Adjutant, Colonel—

COLONEL: I am no better pleased with the Adjutant than I am with yourself in this affair.

ADJUTANT: With your permission, Colonel.

COLONEL: Well?

ADJUTANT: I know that I am justly rebuked . . .

COLONEL: You are, sir.

ADJUTANT: But I cannot in honour say other than that I believe Mister Drake to be right in this affair.

Pause. The COLONEL is shocked.

COLONEL: What did you say?

ADJUTANT: There are certain facts, Colonel, which cannot be denied.

COLONEL: Facts?

ADJUTANT: Yes, Colonel.

COLONEL: You speak to me of facts?

ADJUTANT: . . . I am convinced, Colonel, that Mrs Hasseltine's dress was cut with a sword—

COLONEL: I am not speaking of dresses—

ADJUTANT: And the Doctor himself has given evidence that
Mrs Bandanai was attacked.

    *Pause. The Colonel knows this to be true. And that it was
hidden from him.*

COLONEL: That is a matter that will be looked into.

DRAKE: With respect, Colonel, when did you first hear of
the attack on Mrs Bandanai?

COLONEL: . . . That is no concern of yours.

DRAKE (*hating to do this*): But if you have already been – lied
to once, Colonel—

COLONEL (*quickly*): I have not been lied to! We do not – lie
to one another in this Mess. Gentlemen do not question the
honour of other gentlemen, Mister Drake.

DRAKE: He will attack again, Colonel.

COLONEL: . . . What?

DRAKE: I am convinced that a man who has already attacked
twice, will attack a third time, Colonel. And there are
ladies here who need your protection.

COLONEL: . . . You have not convinced me that this is
the work of one man . . . least of all an officer of this
Regiment.

DRAKE: I believe that I can prove it, with your permission,
Colonel.

COLONEL: . . . How?

DRAKE: By recalling Mrs Hasseltine to the witness chair.

COLONEL: . . . You are suggesting that I should allow this
trial to continue?

DRAKE: I am suggesting, with respect, Colonel, that I can best
serve you and this Regiment by examining this matter here
– where I alone shall suffer if I am mistaken – rather than in
the public forum to which you would be compelled,
Colonel.

    COLONEL *looks at him. Pause.*

COLONEL: You are saying to me that you are prepared to stake your honour on this?

DRAKE: I have no other means of retrieving myself before you, and before this Regiment.

COLONEL: I see. (*Pause.*) And you, Mister Harper? Are you willing to stake twelve years of service on the outcome of this trial?

ADJUTANT (*pause*): I must abide by what I have said to you, Colonel.

COLONEL: Very well. You leave me no alternative. I give you twenty-four hours in which to prove your theories correct. Should you fail, you will not expect to remain with this Regiment. I shall, of course, myself be present, tomorrow night. Good night to you.

ADJUTANT: Good night, Colonel.

He goes. A pause. HARPER *gathers his papers.*

We have hurt a man whom I greatly admire.

DRAKE: I do not know how we can fail to go on doing so.

ADJUTANT: I trust you are aware that I knew nothing of this.

DRAKE: I am . . . yes. Thank you for supporting me, Mister Harper.

ADJUTANT: It is necessary, at all times, to support . . . the honour of the Regiment.

DRAKE: Yes.

ADJUTANT: Well . . . I will say good night to you.

DRAKE: Good night, sir.

ADJUTANT: Good night. (*He goes.*)

Lights fade – PRADAH SINGH *and* WAITERS *enter. One* WAITER *sets a chair for the Colonel down right and moves the Prosecution table and chair upstage. Another* WAITER *sets two chairs up left for the Doctor and Roach. Another* WAITER *sets Mrs Hasseltine's dress under the Defence table. Lights up.*

The Mess. The next night, about 11.30.

WIMBOURNE, V.C. *Officer of the Week, with sword, comes on
with* SECOND-IN-COMMAND, ROACH.

WIMBOURNE: Forget about it, Lionel, stop worrying.

ROACH: I can't, Alastair. This is a wretched business and now
it's wholly out of hand. Besides, I feel responsible.

WIMBOURNE: You, why?

ROACH: If only I had dealt with the matter at the time.

WIMBOURNE: I swear to God, Lionel, you could find a way
to blame yourself for anything that happens in this Regiment.

ROACH: In any case, this kind of trial is a terrible mistake, and
now the Colonel has involved himself personally. (*Pause.*)
I'm going to tell him what I think.

WIMBOURNE: No, Lionel. Take my advice? This is not the
moment. You can only make matters worse, why not wait
and see what happens tonight?

ROACH: . . . All right, Alastair, if you think so.

WIMBOURNE: I do. I do.

ROACH: It's nearly midnight, I'd better fetch him.

WIMBOURNE: Go on then . . . and stop worrying.

    ROACH *goes.* WIMBOURNE *sits on table, thinking.* MRS
HASSELTINE *comes on to veranda.*

MRS HASS: Alastair . . . Alastair . . .

WIMBOURNE: What are you doing here?

MRS HASS: I must speak with you.

    *The whole scene is made doubly urgent by the need for quiet-
ness.*

WIMBOURNE: What the devil's the matter? You shouldn't be
here.

MRS HASS: I've been called again for tonight.

WIMBOURNE: . . . So have I.

MRS HASS: You?

WIMBOURNE: . . . Yes.

MRS HASS: Then they must know . . .

WIMBOURNE: Oh, for God's sake . . .

MRS HASS: But they must, Alastair!

WIMBOURNE: Listen to me. Nobody knows anything! Nobody will discover anything! Just as long as you remain silent.

Pause.

MRS HASS: I don't know that I am any longer prepared to.

WIMBOURNE: What the hell does that mean?

MRS HASS: I have been humiliated once because of you, Alastair. I do not intend to be humiliated again!

WIMBOURNE: Listen to me! You are the last person here who can afford to tell the truth! Remember that!

MRS HASS: Oh . . . What does that mean?

WIMBOURNE: You owe us everything, Marge! Your house, your servants, your land, everything! Without this Regiment, you are nothing.

MRS HASS: I see. Thank you for reminding me of my place in this community.

WIMBOURNE: Marge, you know damn well . . .

MRS HASS: And in your estimation.

COLONEL (*off*): Very well. Gentlemen, I am ready.

He goes via cardroom. She via veranda. The COLONEL *comes on, with* ROACH *and* DOCTOR. *They go to appointed chairs. The Court files on.* DRAKE *and* MILLINGTON *on from down left.*

ADJUTANT: Be seated, gentlemen.

They sit.

This Court is now in session. Mister Drake.

DRAKE (*rises*): I call Mrs Hasseltine, Mister President.

ADJUTANT: Mister Hutton.

HUTTON: Yes, sir.

HUTTON *goes off. Dead silence. He returns with* MRS
HASSELTINE. ADJUTANT *alone rises.*

HUTTON: Would you come in please, ma'am.

ADJUTANT: Be seated, ma'am, please . . .

MRS HASS: . . . Thank you. (*She sits.*)

ADJUTANT: Mister Drake.

DRAKE: Mrs Hasseltine. When I questioned you earlier, you
told me that you had been attacked by Mister Millington –
that you had struck him down with . . . something – and
that you had run into this Mess for fear that he might attack
you again?

MRS HASS: Yes.

DRAKE: Is there anything you wish to add to that statement,
ma'am?

MRS HASS: No.

DRAKE: Is there anything you wish to retract from it?

MRS HASS: No.

DRAKE: You are certain?

MRS HASS: I am.

DRAKE: . . . Very well.

    DRAKE *crouches by his table where the dress has been set. He
    rises with the dress held by the shoulders. He holds it out.*

DRAKE: Do you recognize this, ma'am?

    It is a tremendous shock to her. She stares at it.

Yes, the Indian woman thought it too valuable to burn.
(*Extends the skirt.*) I should like you to look at the skirt,
ma'am.

    She stares at it. Jerks her head round to look up at the court.

I have already explained to the Court, the significance of
this sword-cut.

MRS HASS: . . . I don't understand you.

DRAKE: Very well. (*He throws dress upstage.*) Would you
please look behind you, Mrs Hasseltine?

MRS HASS: . . . What?

DRAKE: Turn around. Look behind you.

MRS HASS: . . . Why?

DRAKE: Are you afraid to?

Very slowly, she turns. There is something strange about this.
What do you see, Mrs Hasseltine?

MRS HASS: ... The plain.

DRAKE: And farther to your left?

MRS HASS: ... The court.

DRAKE: And again farther ... ?

MRS HASS: ... A wall.

DRAKE: What else, Mrs Hasseltine? (*Pause.*) Well ... ?

MRS HASS: ... A showcase.

DRAKE: What is in the showcase?

MRS HASS: ... A tunic.

DRAKE: Whose, Mrs Hasseltine?

She makes a gesture, almost weary, of putting her hands to her
head. Lowering them she turns slowly to DRAKE.

MRS HASS: You know ... ?

DRAKE (*gently*): Yes, ma'am, I know who was there that
night ...

She lowers her head.

I have no wish to distress you, Mrs Hasseltine. I simply
want you to tell us the truth. Will you do that, ma'am?

MRS HASS: Yes ...

DRAKE: Were you attacked by Captain Scarlett?

MRS HASS: ... Yes, I was.

DRAKE: I am sorry, ma'am ...

COLONEL: Mister Drake ...

DRAKE: With respect, Colonel, I believe that all will become
plain in a moment or two. If you will permit me to continue.

COLONEL: ... Very well.

DRAKE: ... I must ask you first, ma'am, whether Mister
Millington attacked you in any serious sense at all?

MRS HASS (*almost amused*): He hasn't the ... violence in him,
Mister Drake.

DRAKE: He did not assault, or ... ?

MRS HASS: He begged me to cry out. He begged me to
accuse him. He was unable to harm me himself.

DRAKE: . . . Do you still wish to bring a complaint against him?

MRS HASS: Of what? Inherent gentleness?

DRAKE: That, surely, is no crime.

MRS HASS: You think not, Mister Drake? Then you are in the wrong place. He is the only gentle man I have met in all my years with this Regiment.

DRAKE: You withdraw the charge before this Court against him?

MRS HASS: I do, yes.

DRAKE: You make no complaint of any kind?

MRS HASS: None whatever.

DRAKE: Thank you, ma'am. I must now ask you about the night of the seventeenth.

MRS HASS: . . . He came so suddenly. Out of the darkness. My name. And then . . . No face. The lights on the Plain. No face . . . (*Absolutely still, calm.*)

DRAKE: . . . He had a sword?

MRS HASS: I tried to run. But I fell. He . . . He cut me. And then . . . he said . . .

DRAKE: . . . What did he say, ma'am?

MRS HASS: He laughed and said . . . 'A point, Marge. A veritable point' . . .

She covers her face with one hand – not weeping. The COLONEL *lowers his head.*

DRAKE: I am sorry to persist in these questions, ma'am. But you have only to tell us who he was . . .

MRS HASS: I don't know who he was . . .

DRAKE: But you must, ma'am . . .

MRS HASS: I don't, Mister Drake . . .

DRAKE: Then why did you accuse Mister Millington, ma'am?

MRS HASS: I had to do something.

DRAKE: Why, Mrs Hasseltine? Unless you recognized your attacker and knew that you could never accuse that man?

MRS HASS: I only knew . . .

DRAKE: What Major Wimbourne chose to tell you?

MRS HASS: I have nothing to say. Nothing.

DRAKE: But . . . his voice, ma'am. You must have recognized his voice.

MRS HASS: It was the voice of John Scarlett . . .

DRAKE: But John Sc . . .

MRS HASS (*terrible amused weariness*): Don't you understand, Mister Drake? It doesn't matter which one of these men it was. They are all the same. Stupid, cruel men, who treat pigs and women as though they were objects . . .

COLONEL (*rises*): Mrs Hasseltine, you are overwrought.

MRS HASS: Colonel. Do you not yet know what you are sire to? They are all John Scarlett. Every one of them.

COLONEL: That will be all, ma'am.

MRS HASS: Yes. (*Nods.*) Oh, yes. (*Crosses to exit.*) It has taken me too long to accept what I have always known. You are scum.

> *She goes. Silence.*

COLONEL: Mister Drake. Explain.

DRAKE: Colonel, there is an officer in this Regiment, who dresses in the uniform worn by this Regiment until shortly after the Mutiny; and in that fashion attacks women.

COLONEL: You must be mistaken.

DRAKE: It is a fact, Colonel. As you have just heard confirmed by Mrs Hasseltine.

COLONEL: Nobody dressed in that manner on the night of the seventeenth.

DRAKE: No, Colonel.

COLONEL: Well, then?

DRAKE: It appears that it is not always necessary.

COLONEL: For what?

DRAKE: The impersonation.

COLONEL: Why would anyone want to impersonate John Scarlett?

DRAKE: With your permission, Colonel, I should like to ask Major Wimbourne.

COLONEL: Very well. Call him.

COLONEL *sits*.

ADJUTANT: Mister Boulton.

BOULTON *goes to cardroom and returns with* WIMBOURNE, V.C.

BOULTON: Would you come this way, please, sir?

WIMBOURNE: About bloody time! (*Attention to Colonel.*) Colonel, sir.

ADJUTANT: Be seated, sir, please.

WIMBOURNE: All right ... Well?

Drake is not impressed by anger – he is as coldly angry himself.

DRAKE: Major Wimbourne, sir. What happened to Mrs Bandanai?

WIMBOURNE: How the hell should I know?

DRAKE: Six months ago Mrs Bandanai was attacked in a particular manner and it was you who took her to the hospital.

WIMBOURNE: Oh, really.

DRAKE: You were seen, sir.

WIMBOURNE: By whom?

DRAKE: The orderlies on duty—

WIMBOURNE: I see ... wogs ...

DRAKE: And by the Doctor.

WIMBOURNE: ... Did he say that?

DRAKE: Do you deny it?

WIMBOURNE: Why should I deny it?

DRAKE: You did take her to the hospital then?

WIMBOURNE: All right – yes I did.

DRAKE: How did that come about?

WIMBOURNE: I found her.

DRAKE: Where, sir?

WIMBOURNE: What the devil does it matter where?

DRAKE: In your bungalow, sir? Is that where you found her?

WIMBOURNE: What if I did?

DRAKE: How did she come to be there?

WIMBOURNE: I haven't the faintest idea.

DRAKE: Had you not asked her to spend the evening with you?

WIMBOURNE: That's no crime.

DRAKE: I didn't say it was, sir.

WIMBOURNE: All right – yes – yes I did.

    COLONEL *reacts*.

DRAKE: Then how did you come to find her, sir? Had you gone out for a walk?

WIMBOURNE: I'd been down to the picquets.

DRAKE: The picquets?

WIMBOURNE: I was Officer of the Week.

DRAKE: I see. And when you came back, you 'found' that she'd been attacked?

WIMBOURNE: Yes. Yes, she had.

DRAKE: How, sir? In what way?

WIMBOURNE: I don't know. I wasn't there.

DRAKE: Was she bleeding, sir?

WIMBOURNE: There was blood on the floor.

DRAKE: Where was she bleeding from?

WIMBOURNE: I don't know. I didn't examine the woman. I took her to the hospital.

    Slight pause.

DRAKE: Did you report this attack to the Colonel, sir?

WIMBOURNE: No.

DRAKE: Why not?

WIMBOURNE: I didn't think it necessary . . . there seemed no point in . . . making trouble . . . for some . . .

DRAKE: Wog?

WIMBOURNE: Yes.

DRAKE: And so by avoiding trouble then, you simply made it later?

WIMBOURNE: What does that mean?

DRAKE: You are aware that Mrs Hasseltine has been attacked?

WIMBOURNE: That's a different thing entirely.

DRAKE: I don't think so, sir. Neither does the Doctor. Nor does Mrs Hasseltine herself.

WIMBOURNE: I don't believe you.

DRAKE: They have both given evidence before this Court, sir. Mrs Hasseltine went further. She identified her attacker.

WIMBOURNE: . . . Mister Millington.

DRAKE: No, sir. Captain John Scarlett.

WIMBOURNE: That's ridiculous! John Scarlett's dead.

DRAKE: I don't think so, sir.

WIMBOURNE: Well, I ought to know! I brought in his remains myself.

DRAKE: Yes, sir, yes, you did.

WIMBOURNE: Well . . . then!

DRAKE: I have been asking myself, sir, what manner of man could have been responsible for attacks of this kind. I should say it was the work of a sportsman, wouldn't you? A man who enjoys his sport.

WIMBOURNE: Why ask me?

DRAKE: Well, who is the champion at 'Making a Point' in this Mess, sir?

WIMBOURNE: There is no champion.

DRAKE: The acknowledged master, then. The outstanding sportsman. The man who scored two goals against the Lancers in the final chukka?

WIMBOURNE: That was me.

DRAKE: Exactly, sir. Indeed it would be fair to say that you epitomize everything that is most admired in this Regiment. You are aggressive, bold, fearless . . .

WIMBOURNE: You don't think I did it?

DRAKE: Why not, sir?

WIMBOURNE: Not me?

DRAKE: I should be interested to hear your reasoning, sir.

    But WIMBOURNE *throws back his head and roars with laughter, real, free laughter.*

I'm glad you find it amusing, sir.

WIMBOURNE: Why don't you examine your own evidence, laddie?

DRAKE: What?

WIMBOURNE (*enjoying himself hugely*): I was right, smack, bang in the middle of the Plain when Marjorie was attacked. I was dancing with Mrs Forster. Everybody saw me!

DRAKE: I don't believe you!

WIMBOURNE: Well, ask him. Ask Fothergill. He took the depositions. It's all written down!

DRAKE: . . . But that can't be true.

WIMBOURNE (*turns*): Mister Harper – ask him.

ADJUTANT: Mister Fothergill?

JUNIOR SUB (*rises*): It's true, Mister Harper. I saw Major Wimbourne myself. And both the Doctor and Mrs Forster have sworn to it in their depositions . . .

WIMBOURNE (*laughing*): Any more bright ideas, laddie?
     A silence. Drake is stunned.

DRAKE: But . . . if it wasn't you . . .

WIMBOURNE: Who was it then? Major Roach?

DRAKE: He was inspecting the picquet . . .

WIMBOURNE: That's right, I saw him. I ran right past him. Was it the Doctor, then?

DRAKE: He was with Major Forster . . .

WIMBOURNE: And I was with Mrs Forster. So you're right back where you started, aren't you?

DRAKE: I don't understand . . .

WIMBOURNE: We seem to have run out of officers.

DRAKE (*quietly to* WIMBOURNE): You know, sir.

WIMBOURNE: What?

DRAKE: You know who Captain Scarlett is.

WIMBOURNE: He's dead.

DRAKE: Sir. If you do nothing, this man will attack again.

WIMBOURNE (*slight hesitation*): Then I must remember to stand with my back to the wall, mustn't I?

DRAKE: Sir . . .

WIMBOURNE (*rises: turns away*): I cannot help you, Mister Drake.

DRAKE: Mister President, I wish to recall the Second-in-Command.

ADJUTANT: Why?

DRAKE: Because he was the last one to see Mrs Hasseltine before she was attacked . . . there is something here that I have missed . . . the man that he almost saw . . .

ROACH: That was just an impression, Mister Drake.

DRAKE: It's all that we have got, sir.

ADJUTANT: Colonel?

COLONEL (*sitting like a stone*): Let him.

ROACH (*rises*): Very well, Colonel.

ADJUTANT: Thank you, Major Wimbourne.

WIMBOURNE: I am sorry, Colonel. There is nothing further that I can tell this Court.

COLONEL: Do not go far, Alastair.

WIMBOURNE: No, Colonel. (*He goes.*)

ADJUTANT: Mister Drake.

DRAKE: Sir. I want to go back to that moment when you entered the Folly, sir . . .

ROACH: Very well . . .

DRAKE: Now it is dark . . . You have just sent Mister Hart to inspect the native quarters . . . The orchestra is playing on the Plain . . . You hear voices . . . Mister Millington pleading, Mrs Hasseltine, angry . . . You step in among the trees . . .

ROACH: . . . Yes . . .

DRAKE: You can't see anything clearly . . . but there is someone . . . very close to you, sir . . . you can sense him . . . you can feel him watching you . . .

ROACH: I can, yes . . .

DRAKE: Where is he, sir . . . ? Where is he?

ROACH: He is . . . behind me . . .

DRAKE: So you turn . . .

    ROACH *half turns. Pause.*

ROACH: . . . It's no use, Mister Drake. I can see no one.

DRAKE: Think, sir. Think!

ROACH: . . . It was just an impression . . .

DRAKE: No, sir, it was a real person, sir . . . It was Captain Scarlett . . .

ROACH: ... I am sorry, Mister Drake ...

DRAKE *bows head in defeat and turns away.*

DRAKE: I see, well ... thank you, sir. Thank you.

ROACH: I am sorry, Mister Drake. I realize now how close I must have been to seeing him.

DRAKE (*tired smile*): We are all close to doing that, sir. But not quite close enough.

ADJUTANT: . . . Have you any further questions, Mister Drake?

DRAKE: No, Mister President. I am sorry, Colonel. I have failed you.

COLONEL (*rises. Tragic dignity*): No, Mister Drake. You have failed neither me, nor yourself. Be seated, please.

He sits. From now on the stricken figure of the Colonel dominates the scene.

Lionel, would you be good enough to send Major Wimbourne to me.

ROACH: Colonel.

He goes. DRAKE *sits, defeated.*

COLONEL: Mister Harper. The purpose of this Court is to pronounce on the guilt or otherwise of Mister Millington. As the charge against him has been withdrawn, that will not long delay you.

ADJUTANT: I can only instruct you, gentlemen, to vote not guilty. Mister Truly.

TRULY: Not guilty, Mister President.

ADJUTANT: Mister Winters.

WINTERS: Not guilty.

ADJUTANT: Mister Hart.

HART: Not guilty.

ADJUTANT: Mister Boulton.

BOULTON: Not guilty.

ADJUTANT: The President also votes not guilty. Mister Millington, rise, please.

MILLINGTON *stands.*

You have been found not guilty by this Court. You are

cleared absolutely as to honour and integrity. You are free to return to your duties. That is all. This Court is dissolved.

COLONEL: Mister Millington. You have been unjustly treated by this Regiment. You have yourself behaved with some stupidity. I trust we may now see a new beginning.

MILLINGTON: ... Yes, Colonel.

COLONEL (*nods*): Very well. I welcome you to this Regiment.

MILLINGTON: Thank you, Colonel.

A pause. COLONEL *turns away.*

ADJUTANT: I congratulate you, Mister Millington.

General congratulations.

COLONEL: Leave us now, please, gentlemen. Mister Drake, you will remain.

ALL '*Colonel* ... *Good night, Colonel*', *etc. As they leave they cluster round Millington shaking his hand, congratulating him.*

HART: Come over to my quarters, we'll have a party, I've got a couple of bottles ...

ADJUTANT: Quietly, gentlemen.

They turn to go, MILLINGTON *turns back.*

MILLINGTON: With your permission, Colonel.

COLONEL: Very well.

MILLINGTON: Thank you, Arthur.

DRAKE: You have nothing to thank me for.

MILLINGTON: I have a bourgeois principle to thank you for.

DRAKE *smiles and they shake hands.*

We may see you later, then.

DRAKE: Perhaps ...

MILLINGTON: Good night, Arthur.

DRAKE: Good night, Millington.

MILLINGTON: Colonel.

COLONEL: Mister Millington.

They go, crowding round Millington.

ADJUTANT: I am sorry, Colonel.

COLONEL: No, Mister Harper. You have behaved as I should

expect of you. With exemplary courage and fairness. You have done well.

ADJUTANT: . . . I would that we had done less well. Good night, Colonel.

COLONEL: Good night . . .

> ADJUTANT *goes.*

DRAKE: I too, take little pleasure in what I have done, Colonel.

COLONEL: You have done what needed to be done. I have this morning received your letter of resignation. Do you wish me to accept it, or to tear it up?

DRAKE: I should like you to accept it. I am sorry, Colonel. I find that I cannot . . . put my honour on to a Regiment. Or on to a man. It is what I am . . . what I do.

COLONEL: In a Regiment, it is necessary to hold one's honour in trust.

DRAKE: I understand that, Colonel.

COLONEL: Very well. I accept your letter of resignation, Mister Drake . . . with regret.

> WIMBOURNE *enters,* COLONEL *sees him.*

Good night, Mister Drake. And thank you.

DRAKE: Good night, Colonel. (*He goes.*)

COLONEL: Alastair . . .

WIMBOURNE: I couldn't tell you, Ben. You'd have been obliged to take official action. The Regiment could never have survived the scandal. What we have hidden has been hidden too long.

COLONEL: I want the matter ended now.

WIMBOURNE: Very well. Leave it to me. It is a matter of honour. It will be settled in the traditional manner.

> *Pause.*

COLONEL: A matter of honour!

WIMBOURNE: It is not as you think, Ben.

COLONEL: Oh, yes. I am the Regiment. What I have allowed to happen, is what I am. It is as well my time here is nearly done. You will not again speak to me of honour. (*He goes.*)

> WIMBOURNE *stands. Suddenly he stiffens. He has thought*

of something. He moves with animal stealth to the veranda. He reaches up and turns down the lamp.

The stage grows darker.

Slowly he looks into the night. The sound of hunting cries, laughter; but strange, not real, echoing distant, as though remembered. WIMBOURNE *returns from the veranda and moves the Prosecution table on stage, brings a lighted oil lamp and places it on table.*

WIMBOURNE *(calls)*: Pradah Singh.

PRADAH: Sahib?

WIMBOURNE: Get these lamps out. Quickly.

PRADAH SINGH begins to go round the room turning down the lamps. The stage grows darker yet. Only the table lamp remains on.

PRADAH: Is there anything further, sahib?

WIMBOURNE: Don't come back.

PRADAH: No, sahib. *(He goes.)*

WIMBOURNE sits at table, gets gun out of his holster, and begins to load it. DRAKE enters in the shadows, from the card-room.

DRAKE: What are you going to do . . . ?

WIMBOURNE looks up. Pause.

WIMBOURNE: You've been very anxious to meet Captain Scarlett, haven't you, Mister Drake? Now you shall.

DRAKE: . . . What?

WIMBOURNE: He's out there now. When I turn down this lamp, he'll come in.

DRAKE *(stares at gun)*: . . . But, why?

WIMBOURNE: Because he always does. We talk together, Mister Drake. He likes to have someone to talk to.

DRAKE: But, sir, you can't . . .

WIMBOURNE: You're very keen on telling us what we can and can't do, aren't you, Mister Drake? And you know nothing. Nothing!

DRAKE: . . . But . . . sir . . .

WIMBOURNE: No! You think this is about honour . . .

DRAKE: Isn't it?

WIMBOURNE: No. It is about ... comradeship. Friendship.

> WIMBOURNE *hesitates, then turns down the table lamp.*
>
> *Intense bright moonlight on the veranda falling from back towards stage.*

Now you will wait in there. You may watch if you wish. But you will not intervene. Do you understand me?

DRAKE: But, sir ... !

WIMBOURNE: Be quiet. Do what you're told.

> *A voice beyond the moonlight. One we have not heard.*
> CAPTAIN SCARLETT.

SCARLETT: Alastair! Are you there, you old rogue?

WIMBOURNE: Get in there – quickly!

DRAKE: ... But ...

WIMBOURNE (*pushing him*): Get in there!

> DRAKE *is forced just inside cardroom arch.*

SCARLETT (*entering on veranda*): Alastair, are you there?

WIMBOURNE: I'm here, John.

> WIMBOURNE *by table, the gun hidden at his side.*
>
> *Intense moonlight.*
>
> *An approach. Booted feet on the veranda. A commanding, faceless figure steps into view. The bright moonlight, coming from behind, hides his face. He wears a shirt and breeches from the 1857 uniform. The boots add inches to his height. The voice is amused, harsh.*

SCARLETT: Well, turn up the lamp, you silly bugger.

> WIMBOURNE *turns up lamp.*

SCARLETT: That's better. Now we can see what we're doing.

> SCARLETT *crosses to showcase, opens it to take out and put on uniform jacket. He has the face of Roach. Yet in all respects he is another man.*

WIMBOURNE: You won't be needing the jacket tonight, John. You won't be going anywhere tonight.

SCARLETT (*laughs*): Why not? Because of that little swine, Lionel Roach? That was a close call, when he started talking about the man he almost saw. He damned nearly

did see me too, the little runt. Damned nearly gave me
away.

WIMBOURNE: That little runt, as you call him, never found
it necessary to attack women.

SCARLETT: Oh, come on, Alastair. Bit of sport! Right in
your country, that is.

WIMBOURNE: No, John.

SCARLETT (*fiercely*): Well no matter! I'm getting stronger,
Alastair . . . I've almost taken over from that little swine
once for all . . .

WIMBOURNE: That's why we must be rid of you now.

SCARLETT: What . . . ?

   WIMBOURNE *fires. The case shatters. The dummy plunges
   out.* SCARLETT *jerks as though shocked, puts hand to head in
   confusion, becomes Roach again, looks at Wimbourne,
   recognizes him.*

ROACH (*puzzled*): Alastair . . . ?

WIMBOURNE: Lionel . . . Look . . . (*He points to showcase.*)
   ROACH *turns, looks at the dummy, stares as though at his own
   dead body.*

ROACH: No! No! (*Tears jacket from himself, throws it to floor.*)
   Oh, God! I saw him! Alastair, I saw him!

   WIMBOURNE *moves centre to join Roach.*

WIMBOURNE: I know.

ROACH: . . . What's wrong with me?

WIMBOURNE: I don't know. It's . . . as though you were . . .
   possessed by him. As though there were . . . two . . .

ROACH: . . . It was me.

WIMBOURNE: No . . . It was . . . you were . . . Scarlett . . .

ROACH (*sits*): Oh, God. It was me.

WIMBOURNE: Lionel . . . Too much damage has been done.
   I can no longer protect you . . . (*He places gun on table.*) Do
   you understand me?

ROACH (*puts his hand on gun*): . . . I understand.

   Pause. WIMBOURNE *puts his hand on the lamp and very
   slowly begins to turn it down.*

WIMBOURNE: . . . I will tell the Colonel that – Captain
Scarlett – is dead.
The lamp is out.
WIMBOURNE *slowly leaves the room.*
A shot in the darkness.

CURTAIN

A NOTE ON ROACH'S ASSUMPTION OF
SCARLETT'S PERSONALITY

In the eighteen fifties, Wimbourne, Roach and Scarlett were subalterns together. Millington's father was then C.O., Drake's a major, the present Colonel perhaps adjutant.

When they were young, Wimbourne was probably hearty, brave and rumbustious, Scarlett similar but vicious, Roach kinder, more thoughtful, more liberal in his outlook. He would have disliked Scarlett but been rather in awe of him.

When they were both taken prisoner, it must have been a matter of mere chance that Scarlett was the first to be flayed alive. Had Wimbourne not come to his rescue, Roach would have undergone the same treatment. So it is reasonable to suppose that in Roach's unconscious mind, the idea was formed that Scarlett had died in his place, that he owed Scarlett a life.

Unconsciously he has allowed Scarlett to come back to life by occupying his body and mind. But Scarlett is the stronger personality, Roach the weaker. And in the battle for occupation of the one available mind and body, Scarlett is winning. He becomes stronger every day, and Roach less and less in control.

It is not to be supposed that Wimbourne understands any of this, that he 'realizes' what is happening to Roach. His reaction is much more simple. Roach is his friend. It is easy to picture the young Wimbourne rather taken by a young man, gentler, more serious, more intelligent than himself. Probably the friendship was protective, and it has grown in strength as time has passed. When Wimbourne sees that Roach is in trouble, he reacts simply: he protects him. And at first this is harmless. But as Scarlett grows stronger, his actions (through Roach) become more outrageous. And in his dilemma,

Wimbourne holds fast to what he believes in; he continues to protect Roach, to stand by his friend.

In this he may be mistaken; but he is brave (for he knows what it costs), and he is himself. At last, compelled to act, he makes it as easy as he can for Roach. But he must kill Scarlett, who has taken Roach over almost completely. So he must kill Roach.